CU00798570

Lynn Chambers trained as a primary school teacher and, after : returned to teaching to specialize in working with children with sp role as a professional teacher, she has over 20 years' experience clubs and Sunday schools. Lynn was Diocesan Children's Officer i 2006. She was ordained in 2004 and served her curacy in Carmartl ......ow Priest-in-Charge of the parishes of Brechfa with Abergorlech and Llanfihangel Rhos-y-corn in West Wales.

Kay Warrington grew up in Swansea and, after living in west Wales and mid Wales for many years, now lives in Ystalyfera, in the Swansea valley. She taught science for nearly 20 years and has worked with children in the church for over 40 years. She was ordained Deacon in 1995, working as a non-stipendiary curate in several parishes. She was Provincial Children and Families Officer (2000–2005) and has been Diocesan Children's Officer for Swansea and Brecon since 1996.

Nia Catrin Williams was ordained in 1998, serving curacies in the parishes of Llanrhos and Colwyn Bay. She was Diocesan Children's Officer for St Asaph Diocese from 2000 to 2003 and full-time Under-25s Officer from 2003 until 2006. Nia is now Vicar in the Ogwen Valley, Diocese of Bangor. She is married to Nigel and they have two daughters.

Published by
The Bible Reading Fellowship
15 The Chambers, Vineyard
Abingdon OX14 3FE
United Kingdom
Tel: +44 (0)1865 319700
Email: enquiries@brf.org.uk
Website: www.brf.org.uk

ISBN 978 1 84101 567 5
First published 2008
10 9 8 7 6 5 4 3 2 1 0

Acknowledgments
Unless otherwise stated, scripture quotations are taken from the Contemporary
English Version of the Bible published by HarperCollins Publishers, copyright ©
1991, 1992, 1995 American Bible Society.

A catalogue record for this book is available from the British Library

Printed in Singapore by Craft Print International Ltd

PLAY and PRAY through Advent

A family resource:
with stories and activities for the
Advent and Christmas season

Lynn Chambers • **Kay Warrington** • **Nia Catrin Williams**

Contributors include past and present members of the Church in Wales Children's Network:
Jayne Ayee
John Davies
Alan Pierce Jones
Angela Williams
Pauline Williams

Important information

Photocopying permission

The right to photocopy material in *Play and Pray through Advent* is granted for the pages that contain the photocopying clause: 'Reproduced with permission from *Play and Pray through Advent* published by BRF 2008 (ISBN 978 1 84101 567 5)', so long as reproduction is for use in a teaching situation by the original purchaser. The right to photocopy material is not granted for anyone other than the original purchaser without written permission from BRF.

The Copyright Licensing Agency (CLA)

If you are resident in the UK and you have a photocopying licence with the Copyright Licensing Agency (CLA) please check the terms of your licence. If your photocopying request falls within the terms of your licence, you may proceed without seeking further permission. If your request exceeds the terms of your CLA licence, please contact the CLA directly with your request: Copyright Licensing Agency, 90 Tottenham Court Rd, London W1T 4LP. Tel 020 7631 5555, fax 020 7631 5500, email cla@cla.co.uk; web www.cla.co.uk. The CLA will provide photocopying authorization and royalty fee information on behalf of BRF.

BRF is a Registered Charity (No. 233280)

Comments from field tests

All the material in this book has been field tested before publication. For your interest and encouragement, here are some of the comments that were subsequently fed back to the authors.

'Monday Club meets during the lunch break. Led by a team of five members of local churches, it is open to anyone who wishes to join in at any time. The aim is to learn about the Christian faith and about caring for one another and for all of God's creation, through stories, songs, craft, puzzles and games. It is intended to be a time of fun as well as a considering time. *Play and Pray through Advent* has helped us to explore Bible stories in a simple visual way and talk about our understanding of God. We have prayed together and sung together and crafted reminders of what we have shared to take home. The resource was easily adapted to suit the situation and the time that is available to us.'
(Knelston School, Swansea and Brecon)

'This method of teaching was completely new to people in our congregation and the response has been amazing. The story cloth earned respect and was considered a sacred space. The children all responded well and discussions were sometimes very funny and at other times quite touching. As a new teacher, I am learning so much myself through *Play and Pray through Advent*. Truly, for me, it has been a Godsend.'
(St Paul's Llansamlet, Swansea and Brecon)

'We used *Play and Pray through Advent* with our children's craft group which meets on Saturday morning and it has been great fun for us and the children. Well done for creating a programme appropriate for those with experience and those just starting out on their journey, working with children in the church.'
(Llysfaen, St Asaph)

'We were absolutely delighted to pilot *Play and Pray through Advent* with our midweek club as it did 'exactly what it said on the tin'. The diversity of the craftwork was excellent, the stories first class and the songs to familiar tunes very easy to pick up. The proof of the pudding, though, is in the eating and our children thoroughly enjoyed all the different aspects of the course. I am delighted to say that I can commend it to colleagues in Sunday school, junior church and, as in our case, midweek club.'
(Aberedw, Swansea and Brecon)

Contents

Foreword

If you wish to communicate the gospel of our Lord Jesus Christ in your family, primary school, Sunday school or children's club, you have an immensely valuable resource in your hands.

A good deal of what is here is based on the idea of *Godly Play*. This was in many ways a new concept at a time when ever more sophisticated media were being tried in the classroom and church. In contrast, *Godly Play* emphasizes the telling of stories and the vital component of human interaction. That interaction is not simply between storyteller and 'audience' (a better word would be 'participants') but also between the participants themselves.

The fundamental concept has much in common with good liturgical practice. Effective public worship is unself-conscious; it's about a conversation and a relationship between a congregation (including its leader) and God. When a congregation celebrates, let's say, Christmas, it's not simply celebrating the anniversary of the birth of Christ—that would be to turn Christmas into nothing more than a birthday celebration. Good liturgy invites the congregation back to Bethlehem, to experience afresh the tent-pitching of the divine Word among us, and leads us to pray that Christ may be 'born in us today'. That's the way this book works: it invites all its participants to bring the stories of the gospel to life in themselves.

The book is full of great ideas to suit every context in which it may be used and, most importantly, it links with the worship of the church. Far too much activity with children in church is tokenism. We shuffle them off somewhere else to be creative; then, when they are nicely wound up, we bring them back for a blessing at a moment in the service when the adults are at their most spiritually focused. Result: frustration for the children, annoyance for the adults. This book provides the material for vitally blurring the age-divide, allowing children to share with adults at least a little of what they are discovering of the gospel, and encouraging adults to share with children a little of what they, too, are experiencing of God.

I remember having a copy of the pilot version of this book and being most impressed with it, not least because I had first-hand experience that its compilers know what they're writing about. I hope you'll want to share this book with others: why not get some copies for friends with children of primary school age or for children's group leaders?

Robert Paterson, Bishop of Sodor and Mann
(Formerly Principal Officer of the Church in Wales Council for Mission and Ministry, 2000–2006)

Introduction

Play and Pray through Advent unites the world of the child with the themes we experience in church during the period of Advent and Christmastide. This innovative programme, based on the Revised Common Lectionary, suggests ways in which children can engage creatively with the story at home or in midweek groups and clubs, by exploring themes from the Gospels and preparing for the Sunday worship of their local church.

The material is based on the methodology of *Godly Play*, using story cloths and simple visuals to tell the story. *Godly Play* is a teaching method developed by Jerome Berryman in the United States. Play is nature's way of extending the child's horizons and understanding of life. The *Godly Play* approach draws on this natural sense of playfulness and creativity to enable the spiritual growth of the child.

Advent and Christmastide

Play and Pray through Advent encourages children and families to participate in the events surrounding the birth of Jesus, his early years and the beginning of his ministry. During the four Sundays of Advent, Christians get ready for Christmas by reflecting on how the birth of the Saviour was heralded in the Old Testament scriptures and the New Testament Gospels. Messages were brought by the prophets, John the Baptist and angels.

Christmas celebrates the birth of the promised Saviour. After Christmas we celebrate the visit of the wise men and the presentation of Christ in the temple (known as Candlemas and celebrated on 2 February in some church traditions), when we celebrate the presentation of the Christ-child in the temple and his recognition as the light for the world. The story of the presentation of Christ in the temple ends the 40 days of Christmas and Epiphany. This story is a pivotal feast between Christmas and Easter, when Christians look back again at Christmas before turning towards the cross.

How to use this book

This programme enables families to prepare in a creative way for the worship each Sunday and may also be used in Sunday school, midweek clubs, children's groups or circle time in primary schools. Each week has a double-page spread comprising three distinct sections:

Getting ready

- ✪ Theme for the week
- ✪ Bible focus, providing the background for the story cloth activities
- ✪ Story for the week, telling the Gospel story in simple language

Let's play and pray...

- ✪ Story cloth activities for each day of the week
- ✪ Talk-about ideas, suggesting daily topics to talk about together
- ✪ Prayer for the week to end each day's activity

Song for the week

On pages 50–67, you will find suggestions for a song for each week, which may be sung at home as part of the daily activities and also incorporated into the Sunday worship. The songs are all sung to well-known nursery rhymes or other popular melodies.

Craft for the week

On pages 70–74, simple crafts have been suggested, primarily for those who are completing the week's activities in one session. The cloth would be used to tell the story, using the appropriate artefacts. This would be followed up with 'Talk about' and the prayer and song for the week, then lead into the craft activity.

Celebrating on Sunday

- ✪ Take-to-church suggestions for items to be brought to church each Sunday
- ✪ Sunday worship suggestions for how the minister or worship leader might link the project into the Sunday worship. This may take place at any appropriate point in the service and could be used as the sermon slot. The prayer for the week may be used in addition to, or in place of, the Sunday Collect.

Practical points

You will need:

- ✪ a small box
- ✪ a circle of purple-coloured cloth (Advent), 70cm in diameter
- ✪ a circle of gold-coloured cloth (Christmas and Epiphany), 70cm in diameter
- ✪ a circle of white-coloured cloth (Epiphany to Candlemas), 70cm in diameter
- ✪ a space set aside at home to carry out the story cloth activities
- ✪ a larger space in church or junior church
- ✪ card copies of the templates
- ✪ scissors
- ✪ felt-tipped pens
- ✪ Blu-tack

As the programme develops, the circular coloured cloths should be placed so that they overlap, as below.

The cloths and other items may be stored in the small box and laid out each day. However, if room allows, the relevant cloth should be left on display throughout the project, providing a 'special' or 'sacred' space in the home. Similarly, in church, this 'special' or 'sacred' space may be maintained throughout the programme so that anyone entering the building may witness the church's journey through Advent and Christmas to the presentation of Christ in the temple (Candlemas).

When to start and finish

You will need to start *Play and Pray through Advent* on the Monday of the week before Advent Sunday.

The programme provides for four Sundays in Epiphany, but in some years this fourth Sunday will not be used. The last week of the programme should always be 'The presentation of Christ in the temple (Candlemas)', which falls on 2 February.

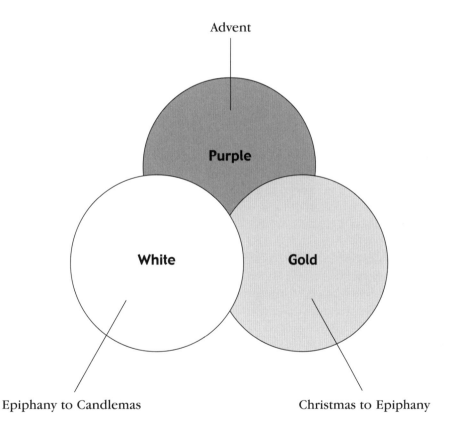

Advent — Purple

White — Epiphany to Candlemas

Gold — Christmas to Epiphany

First week of Advent

 Getting ready

Theme

Jesus tells us to get ready

Bible focus

Always be ready! You don't know when the Son of Man will come.

MATTHEW 24:44

Story for the week

Advent is the time for getting ready. It is the four weeks when we prepare for Christmas. We think about Jesus coming to us as a baby, and we think about Jesus coming again. Long, long ago, God made a promise. God promised that one day he would send Jesus back to us as a glorious king. Also, God said that he would send angels to his people (Mark 13:27). No one knows the day or the time, but God wants us to be ready for when Jesus comes. To be ready, we must keep on praying to God.

 Let's play and pray...

 Story cloth activities

Monday

One day Jesus will come to us as a king.

Cut out the candle with a crown from the template on page 76 and place it on the purple cloth.

Tuesday

Jesus will come in glory.

Cut out the candle with a trumpet from the template on page 76 and place it on the cloth.

Wednesday

God made a promise long ago.

Cut out the candle with a scroll from the template on page 77 and place it on the cloth.

Thursday

God will send angels to his people.

Cut out the candle with an angel from the template on page 77 and place it on the cloth.

Friday

God told us to be ready.

Cut out and colour the 'get ready' card from the template on page 77 and place it on the cloth.

Saturday

God told us to keep praying.

Light a tealight candle and put it by the candle with a crown.

Talk about

Monday	I wonder what it feels like to meet a king.
Tuesday	What do you think 'glory' means?
Wednesday	Talk about keeping promises.
Thursday	Have you ever had to give someone an important message?
Friday	Talk about getting ready.
Saturday	Where is a good place to pray?

 Prayer for the week

Loving God, you asked us to get ready. Help us to be ready to celebrate the event of Jesus' birth. Amen

Song for the week

Wait with us (Tune: Jingle bells)
See page 50.

— Years A–C —

First week of Advent

Tune: Jingle Bells

Wait with us, wait with us,
Wait with us and pray,
For we know the Son of God
Will come to us again.

Oh!
He is king, we will sing
On this happy day!
Wait with us, wait with us,
Wait with us and pray.

Sing with us, sing with us,
Sing with us today,
For we know the Son of God
Will come to us again.

Oh!
He is king, we will sing
On this happy day!
Wait with us, wait with us,
Wait with us and pray.

 ## Celebrating on Sunday

The first Sunday of Advent

Take to church

Take to church the 'get ready' card.

Sunday worship

For the minister or worship leader

> **You will need:**
> ✪ extra 'get ready cards' for everyone in the congregation

During the service

The minister or worship leader may explore and develop the talking points, then say the prayer for the week, inviting people to bring 'get ready' cards to place on the cloth. The children may end this time by singing the song for the week (see page 50).

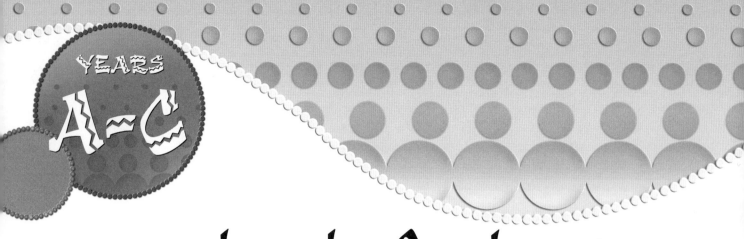

Second week of Advent

 **Getting ready**

 Let's play and pray...

Theme

A messenger is coming

Bible focus

It began just as God had said in the book written by Isaiah the prophet, 'I am sending my messenger to get the way ready for you.'

MARK 1:2

Story for the week

Long, long ago, there was a prophet called Isaiah, who wrote a book that is in the Old Testament part of the Bible. It is called the book of Isaiah. In this book, Isaiah says that God will send a messenger who will come from the stony desert and bring us good news about a Saviour. In the New Testament, we are told that the messenger will be called John the Baptist. John will help people to get ready for Jesus. He will clear the way for Jesus, just like clearing away stones to make a straight path through the desert. We must get ready, too. We must be sorry for the wrong things we do, think or say and must live in a way that pleases God.

 Story cloth activities

Monday

A long time ago, the prophet Isaiah wrote a book.

Cut out and colour the open book shape from the template on page 78.

Tuesday

Isaiah said, 'God is sending a messenger.'

Cut out the messenger shape from the template on page 78 and place it next to the book.

Wednesday

The messenger is John and he brings good news about Jesus.

Cut out and colour the word 'Jesus' from the template on page 78 and place it on the book.

Thursday

The messenger will come from the desert.

Use some stones to make a stony desert.

Friday

The messenger says, 'Clear the way for Jesus.'

Clear a path through the stones.

Saturday

The messenger says we should say 'sorry'.

Say a sorry prayer. Light a tealight candle and place by the candle with a trumpet.

Talk about

Monday	Talk about your favourite Bible story.
Tuesday	How do you think the messenger felt?
Wednesday	What is the best news you have ever had?
Thursday	Talk about what it is like to live in the desert.
Friday	Talk about what paths are for.
Saturday	Why should we say sorry to God?

Prayer for the week

Loving God, your messenger brought good news of Jesus. Help us to share the good news with others. Amen

Song for the week

Isaiah wrote a book (Tune: One man went to mow)
See page 51.

--- Years A–C ---

Second week of Advent

Tune: One man went to mow

Isaiah wrote a book, a long,
long time ago.
Isaiah wrote a book, a long,
long time ago.

A messenger, he said,
will come out from the desert.
A messenger, he said,
will come out from the desert.

The messenger will come
to clear the way for Jesus.
The messenger will come
to clear the way for Jesus.

'Get ready all,' he said,
for Jesus brings us good news.
'Get ready, all,' he said,
for Jesus brings us good news.

'We are sorry' they said,
'for the bad things we've done.'
'We are sorry,' they said,
'for the bad things we've done.'

Isaiah wrote a book, a long,
long time ago.
Isaiah wrote a book, a long,
long time ago.

Celebrating on Sunday

The second Sunday of Advent

Take to church

Take to church one of the stones from the desert.

Sunday worship

For the minister or worship leader

You will need:
✪ extra stones for everyone in the congregation

During the service

The minister or worship leader may explore and develop the talking points, then say the prayer for the week, inviting people to bring stones to place on the cloth. The children may end this time by singing the song for the week (see page 51).

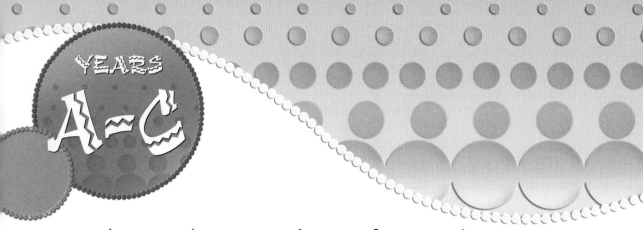

Third week of Advent

Getting ready

Theme

John tells about Jesus

Bible focus

God sent a man named John, who came to tell about the light and to lead all people to have faith.

JOHN 1:6–7

Story for the week

God has sent a messenger to us. He is called John the Baptist. He lives alone in the desert. John wears clothes made out of camel's hair, with a leather strap around his waist. His food is locusts, which are a kind of grasshopper, and honey. John baptizes people and says that everyone has to make a clean start. He takes them down into the water as a sign that they are sorry for the things they have thought, said or done wrong. He tells the people about Jesus. John says that Jesus is greater than him. Jesus is like a light shining in the darkness to show us the way to God.

Let's play and pray...

Story cloth activities

Monday

The messenger is John the Baptist.

Cut out the John the Baptist figure from the template on page 79 and colour him in. Take the messenger shape away and put John in its place.

Tuesday

John baptizes people in water.

Put a little container of water next to John.

Wednesday

John says that people have to make a clean start.

Clean one of the stones in the water.

Thursday

John tells people about Jesus.

Move the word 'Jesus' next to John.

Friday

John says that Jesus is greater than him.

Take John away and keep him for later.

Saturday

John says that Jesus is like a light shining in the dark.

Light a tealight candle and place by the candle with a scroll.

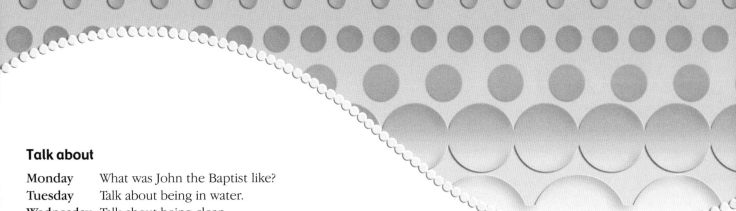

Talk about

Monday	What was John the Baptist like?
Tuesday	Talk about being in water.
Wednesday	Talk about being clean.
Thursday	What could you tell people about Jesus?
Friday	What makes Jesus great?
Saturday	Talk about darkness and light.

🙏 Prayer for the week

Loving God, you sent Jesus as the light for the world. Help us to show his light in our lives. Amen

Song for the week

What was John the Baptist like? (Tune: London Bridge is falling down)
See page 52.

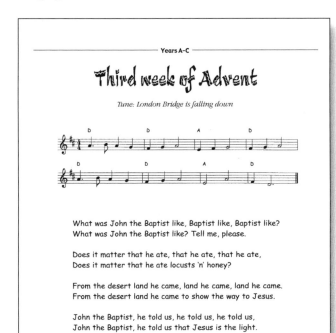

— Years A–C —

Third week of Advent

Tune: London Bridge is falling down

What was John the Baptist like, Baptist like, Baptist like?
What was John the Baptist like? Tell me, please.

Does it matter that he ate, that he ate, that he ate,
Does it matter that he ate locusts 'n' honey?

From the desert land he came, land he came, land he came.
From the desert land he came to show the way to Jesus.

John the Baptist, he told us, he told us, he told us,
John the Baptist, he told us that Jesus is the light.

Celebrating on Sunday

The third Sunday of Advent

Take to church

Take to church a tealight candle.

Sunday worship

For the minister or worship leader

> **You will need:**
> ✪ extra tealight candles for everyone in the congregation

During the service

The minister or worship leader may explore and develop the talking points, then say the prayer for the week, inviting people to bring tealight candles to place on the cloth. The children may end this time by singing the song for the week (see page 52).

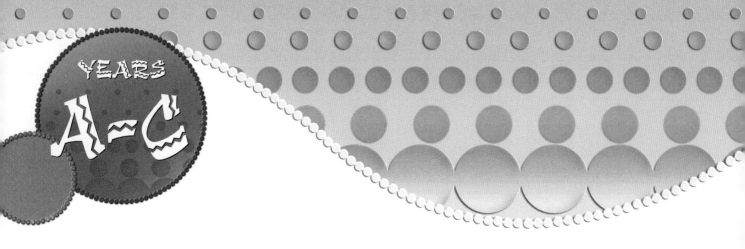

Fourth week of Advent

 Getting ready

 Let's play and pray...

Theme

Mary will have a baby

Bible focus

A virgin will have a baby boy, and he will be called Immanuel, which means 'God is with us.'
MATTHEW 1:23

Story for the week

Mary and Joseph live in Galilee. Mary and Joseph are engaged to be married. One day, when Mary is on her own, she feels that someone is standing near her. She is scared to see an angel, but the angel says, 'Don't be afraid.' The angel tells her some surprising news. She will have a baby and call him Jesus. Joseph is very worried about this, but an angel visits him too. This angel comes to him in a dream. The angel says that the baby is God's Son. Mary and Joseph are both happy and Mary sings a song of praise.

Story cloth activities

Monday
Mary and Joseph live in Galilee.
   Cut out the figure of Mary from the template on page 80, colour her in and put her on the book shape.

Tuesday
An angel visits Mary.
   Put some glittery tinsel next to Mary to show the angel.

Wednesday
The angel says that Mary will have a baby called Jesus.
   Put the word 'Jesus' on Mary.

Thursday
Joseph is worried.
   Cut out the figure of Joseph from the template on page 80, colour him in and put him on the cloth.

Friday
An angel tells Joseph that the baby is God's Son.
   Put the tinsel next to Joseph.

Saturday
Mary sings a song of praise.
   Light a tealight candle and place it by the candle with the angel.

Talk about

Monday   Talk about where you live.
Tuesday   What do you think angels are like?
Wednesday Do you know any babies?
Thursday   Do you worry about things?
Friday   How did Joseph feel?
Saturday   What's your favourite song or hymn?

 Prayer for the week

Loving God, you sent an angel to Mary to tell her about Jesus. Help us to know and love him like she did. Amen

Song for the week

One day Mary was alone (Tune: Frère Jacques)
See page 53.

— Years A–C —

Fourth week of Advent

Tune: Frère Jacques

[musical notation]

One day Mary, one day Mary was alone, was alone.
An angel came to see her, an angel came to see her
with some news, with some news.

Listen Mary, listen Mary. God is pleased, God is pleased.
You will have a baby, you will have a baby.
What great news, what great news!

Joseph's worried, Joseph's worried. What to do? What to do?
An angel came to see him, an angel came to see him
with some news, with some news.

Name him Jesus, name him Jesus. He's God's Son, he's God's Son.
His name means 'God is with us', his name means 'God is with us'.
What good news, what good news!

Celebrating on Sunday

The fourth Sunday of Advent

Take to church

Take to church your 'tinsel angel'.

Sunday worship

For the minister or worship leader

> You will need:
> ✪ extra tinsel for everyone in the congregation

During the service

The minister or worship leader may explore and develop the talking points, then say the prayer for the week, inviting people to bring 'tinsel angels' to place on the cloth. The children may end this time by singing the song for the week (see page 53).

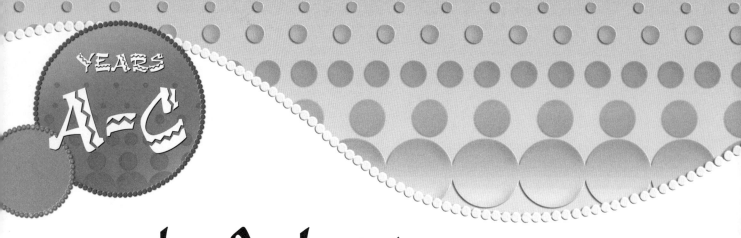

Week of Christmas

Getting ready

Christmas Day may fall any time in this week.

Theme

Jesus is born

Bible focus

This very day in King David's home town a Saviour was born for you.

LUKE 2:11

Story for the week

Mary and Joseph travel to Bethlehem to be counted by the Roman soldiers. There are so many people there that Mary and Joseph have nowhere to stay. Mary is about to have her baby and she is very tired. They find a stable behind the inn. Jesus is born and Mary puts him in a bed of straw. Mary and Joseph are very happy.

Shepherds are out in the fields with their sheep. Angels come to tell them that the baby has been born. The shepherds run down to Bethlehem to see this special baby. Jesus, the light, has come into our world to give light to everyone.

Let's play and pray...

Story cloth activities

Monday

Mary and Joseph go to Bethlehem to be counted.

Cut out and colour the Bethlehem shape from the template on page 81 and place it on the cloth. Place Mary and Joseph next to it.

Tuesday

Jesus is born.

Put a gold cloth next to the purple one.

Wednesday

Jesus is placed in a bed of straw.

Make a manger out of some yellow paper, straw or wool and place it on the gold cloth.

Thursday

Mary and Joseph are happy.

Move Mary and Joseph next to the manger.

Friday

Visitors come to see Jesus.

Cut out and colour the sheep and shepherd shapes from the template on page 81 and place them on the gold cloth.

Saturday

The light has come into the world.

Light a tealight candle and put it in a saucer on the manger.

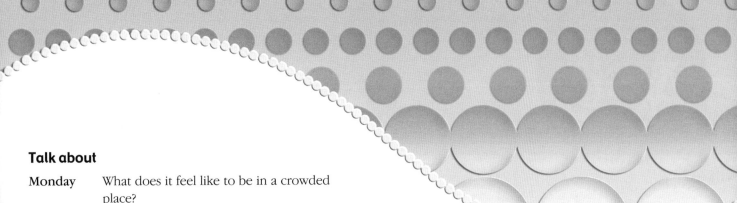

Talk about

Monday	What does it feel like to be in a crowded place?
Tuesday	Talk about the colour gold.
Wednesday	What do you think a bed of straw feels like?
Thursday	Talk about feeling happy.
Friday	How do you feel when people visit you?
Saturday	Talk about the light that Jesus brings.

Prayer for the week

Loving God, Mary and Joseph had nowhere to stay. Help us to find a place for Jesus in our hearts. Amen

Song for the week

We're going to see a baby (Tune: We wish you a merry Christmas)
See page 54.

— Years A–C —

Week of Christmas

Tune: We wish you a merry Christmas

We're going to see a baby,
We're going to see a baby,
Yes we're going to see a baby,
And we're told he's a king!

He's lying in a manger,
He's lying in a manger,
Yes he's lying in a manger
In Bethlehem's town!

It seems like strange behaviour,
But the one we call the Saviour
Was a baby in a manger,
When he's really a king.

So let's sing out our praises
With the shepherds and the angels
For the child born in the stable,
Lord Jesus, our king.

Celebrating on Sunday

The week of Christmas

Take to church

Take to church a piece of wool or straw from your manger.

Sunday worship

For the minister or worship leader

You will need:
✪ extra pieces of wool or straw for everyone in the congregation

During the service

The minister or worship leader may explore and develop the talking points, then say the prayer for the week, inviting people to bring pieces of wool or straw to place on the cloth to make a manger. The children may end this time by singing the song for the week (see page 54).

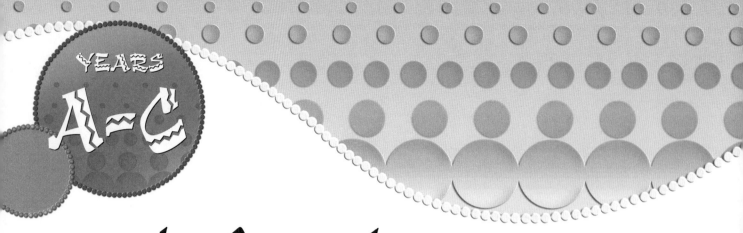

Week after Christmas

Getting ready

Theme
Mary and Joseph name Jesus

Bible focus
And they named him Jesus, just as the angel had told Mary.

LUKE 2:21b

Story for the week
Angels tell the shepherds that Jesus has been born. The shepherds hurry down to Bethlehem. They find the stable and see the baby lying in a bed of straw. They tell Mary that Jesus is the Saviour of the world. The shepherds are so excited about the baby that they praise God and run around telling everyone the news. Mary quietly thinks and wonders about all that is happening to her. Eight days later, Mary and Joseph take their baby to the Jewish meeting place. They name their baby Jesus, just as the angel had said.

Let's play and pray...

Story cloth activities

Monday
The shepherds tell Mary that Jesus is the Saviour of the world.
   Take away the tealight candle and saucer. Cut the baby shape from the template on page 82, colour it in and place it in the manger.

Tuesday
The shepherds praise God.
   Make a paper streamer.

Wednesday
The shepherds go out and tell everyone.
   Move the shepherds to the edge of the cloth.

Thursday
Mary thinks and wonders.
   Move Mary to be on her own.

Friday
Mary and Joseph take Jesus to the Jewish meeting place.
   Move Joseph and Jesus to be with Mary.

Saturday
They name their baby Jesus.
   Move the word 'Jesus' and place it on the baby.

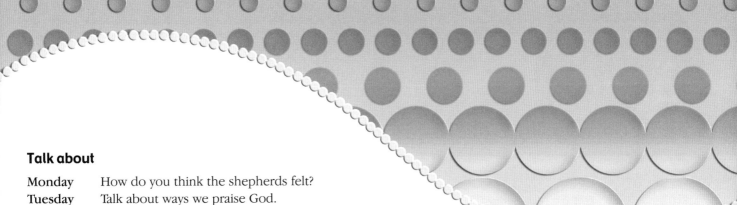

Talk about

Monday	How do you think the shepherds felt?
Tuesday	Talk about ways we praise God.
Wednesday	Talk about telling people news.
Thursday	Talk about times when you have thought and wondered about things.
Friday	Talk about going to church for special services.
Saturday	Talk about your own names and how you got them.

 Prayer for the week

Loving God, your Son was given the special name of Jesus. Help us to remember that all our names are special to you. Amen

Song for the week

What's the name of your baby? (Tune: There's a hole in my bucket)
See page 55.

— Years A–C —

Week after Christmas

Tune: There's a hole in my bucket

(Two-part song for Mary and the shepherds)

What's the name of your baby,
dear Mary, dear Mary?
What's the name of your baby,
dear Mary, what name?

We are calling him Jesus,
dear shepherds, dear shepherds.
We are calling him Jesus,
he's born to be king.

What a strange name to give him,
dear Mary, dear Mary.
What a strange name to give him.
Where did that come from?

From an angel named Gabriel,
dear shepherds, dear shepherds.
From an angel named Gabriel,
he gave me the name.

We have also seen angels,
dear Mary, dear Mary.
We have also seen angels
while watching our sheep.

You're the first to see Jesus,
dear shepherds, dear shepherds.
You're the first to see Jesus
asleep in the hay.

We'll all tell the good news,
dear Mary, dear Mary.
We'll all tell the good news that
we have seen the king.

Celebrating on Sunday

The week after Christmas

Take to church

Take to church the word 'Jesus'.

Sunday worship

For the minister or worship leader

You will need:
* ✪ extra 'Jesus' words for everyone in the congregation

During the service

The minister or worship leader may explore and develop the talking points, then say the prayer for the week, inviting people to bring the 'Jesus' words to place on the cloth. The children may end this time by singing the song for the week (see page 55).

Week of Epiphany (Option 1)

 Getting ready

 Let's play and pray...

Theme

The wise men visit Jesus

Bible focus

They took out their gifts of gold, frankincense, and myrrh and gave them to Jesus.

MATTHEW 2:11b

Story for the week

Wise men who are living in a country to the east of Judea see a new star in the sky. They wonder if it means that a new king has been born. They ride on their camels, following the star across the desert. They come to Jerusalem and ask King Herod if he knows about a newborn king. Herod is jealous and upset. His advisers say that long ago God promised a king, to be born in Bethlehem. King Herod tells the wise men, 'Go and look in Bethlehem and then tell me where to find the baby.' The star leads the wise men to Jesus. They kneel down and give the baby special gifts of gold, frankincense and myrrh. They don't tell Herod but go back to their own homes.

 Story cloth activities

Monday

Wise men come to Jerusalem looking for a baby king.

Cut out the three wise men from the template on page 83, colour them in and place them on the cloth.

Tuesday

The wise men have followed a star.

Cut out the star from the template on page 83, colour it in and place it in front of the wise men.

Wednesday

King Herod is jealous and upset.

Make a grumpy face from card and place it beside the wise men.

Thursday

King Herod tells the wise men to look in Bethlehem.

Move the star and the wise men forward to Jesus.

Friday

They find Jesus and give him gifts.

Cut out and colour the gift shapes from the template on page 83, colour them in and place them by Jesus.

Saturday

The wise men go back to their own homes.

Remove the wise men and the grumpy face.

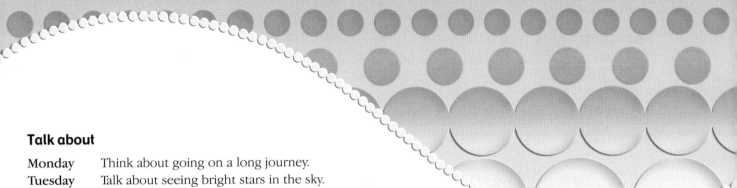

Talk about

Monday	Think about going on a long journey.
Tuesday	Talk about seeing bright stars in the sky.
Wednesday	What does it feel like to be jealous?
Thursday	How do you think the wise men felt when they found Jesus?
Friday	Why do we sometimes take a gift when we visit people?
Saturday	What does it feel like, coming home after a long journey?

Prayer for the week

Loving God, the wise men followed the star to Jesus. Help us to follow Jesus in our lives. Amen

Song for the week

Wise men travelled from afar (Tune: Twinkle, twinkle, little star)
See page 56.

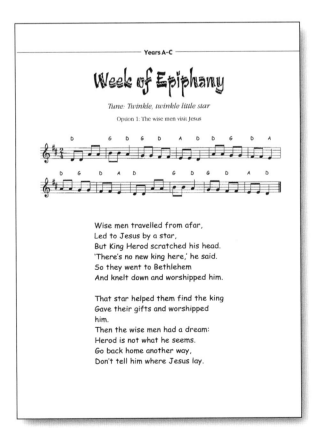

Years A–C

Week of Epiphany

Tune: Twinkle, twinkle little star

Option 1: The wise men visit Jesus

Wise men travelled from afar,
Led to Jesus by a star,
But King Herod scratched his head.
'There's no new king here,' he said.
So they went to Bethlehem
And knelt down and worshipped him.

That star helped them find the king
Gave their gifts and worshipped him.
Then the wise men had a dream:
Herod is not what he seems.
Go back home another way,
Don't tell him where Jesus lay.

 ## Celebrating on Sunday

The week of Epiphany

Take to church

Take to church a 'gift' shape.

Sunday worship

For the minister or worship leader

You will need:
- ✪ extra gift shapes for everyone in the congregation

During the service

The minister or worship leader may explore and develop the talking points, then say the prayer for the week, inviting people to bring the 'gift' shape to place on the cloth. The children may end this time by singing the song for the week (see page 56).

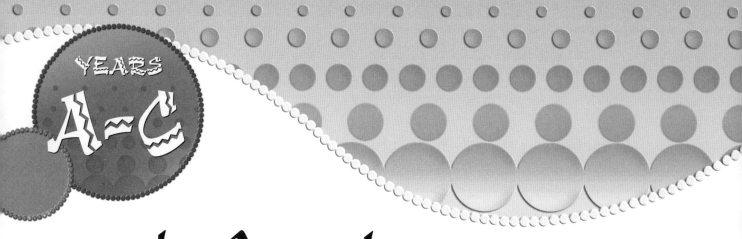

Week of Epiphany (Option 2)

 ## Getting ready

 ## Let's play and pray...

Theme

Jesus is baptized in the River Jordan

Bible focus

Then a voice from heaven said, 'This is my own dear Son, and I am pleased with him.'

MATTHEW 3:17

Story for the week

The baby Jesus grows up and becomes a man. One day, Jesus comes from Galilee and goes down to the River Jordan. John the Baptist is baptizing people. He takes the people down into the water to be washed clean from their sins. Jesus says, 'Baptize me.' John knows that Jesus is already clean from sin. At first, he doesn't want to baptize Jesus, but Jesus insists. Then everyone watches as John baptizes Jesus. Jesus goes down into the water and, when he comes up again, God's Spirit comes down on him like a dove. They hear God's voice saying, 'This is my own dear Son, and I am pleased with him.'

Story cloth activities

Monday
Jesus leaves Galilee.
 Cut out Jesus from the template on page 84, colour him in and place him on the cloth. (Take away the baby Jesus and the word 'Jesus'.)

Tuesday
Jesus goes to the River Jordan.
 Make a river out of blue ribbon, paper or felt, and place it on the cloth.

Wednesday
Jesus asks John to baptize him.
 Place the John the Baptist figure back on the cloth.

Thursday
Jesus goes down into the water.
 Place John and Jesus in the river.

Friday
God's Spirit comes down as a dove.
 Cut out a dove from the template on page 84 and place it above Jesus.

Saturday
God says, 'I am pleased with Jesus, my Son.'
 Make a smiley face from card and place it next to Jesus.

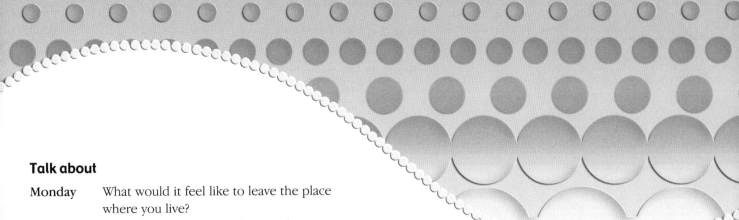

Talk about

Monday	What would it feel like to leave the place where you live?
Tuesday	Talk about the sounds a river makes.
Wednesday	Talk about being baptized.
Thursday	Talk about how we use water.
Friday	Why is God's Spirit like a dove?
Saturday	What does it feel like when people say nice things about you?

Prayer for the week

Loving God, you said that you were pleased with Jesus. Help us to live lives pleasing to you. Amen

Song for the week

Jesus came down from Galilee (Tune: The wheels on the bus)
See page 57.

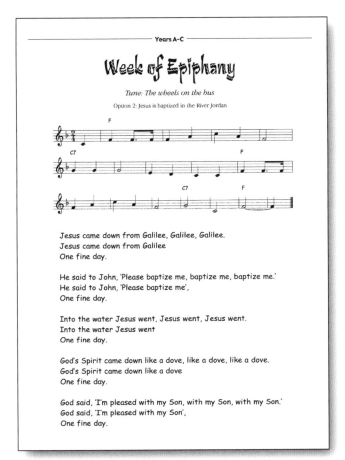

Years A–C

Week of Epiphany

Tune: The wheels on the bus

Option 2: Jesus is baptized in the River Jordan

Jesus came down from Galilee, Galilee, Galilee.
Jesus came down from Galilee
One fine day.

He said to John, 'Please baptize me, baptize me, baptize me.'
He said to John, 'Please baptize me',
One fine day.

Into the water Jesus went, Jesus went, Jesus went.
Into the water Jesus went
One fine day.

God's Spirit came down like a dove, like a dove, like a dove.
God's Spirit came down like a dove
One fine day.

God said, 'I'm pleased with my Son, with my Son, with my Son.'
God said, 'I'm pleased with my Son',
One fine day.

Celebrating on Sunday

The week of Epiphany

Take to church

Take to church a piece of your river.

Sunday worship

For the minister or worship leader

You will need:
✪ extra pieces of blue paper or fabric for everyone in the congregation

During the service

The minister or worship leader may explore and develop the talking points, then say the prayer for the week, inviting people to bring pieces of blue paper or fabric to make a big river on the cloth. The children may end this time by singing the song for the week (see page 57).

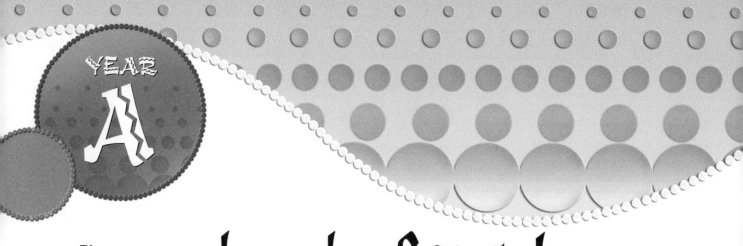

Second week of Epiphany

Getting ready

Theme

John's disciples follow Jesus

Bible focus

He is the one I told you about when I said... 'He is greater than I am.'

JOHN 1:30a

Story for the week

One day, John the Baptist is walking along with his two friends when he sees Jesus. John says to them, 'Look, there is the Lamb of God! I told you about him. He's more important than me.' The two friends follow Jesus, who turns and asks, 'What do you want?' They reply, 'Teacher, where do you live?' Jesus says, 'Come and see.' They go and spend the rest of the day talking with Jesus. One of the friends, called Andrew, goes back and tells his brother, Simon, 'We have found the Messiah.' Andrew takes Simon to see Jesus. Jesus gives Simon a new name. He calls him Peter.

Let's play and pray...

Story cloth activities

Monday

John the Baptist is walking with his friends.

Put down the white cloth next to the other two cloths. Take John out of the river and place him on the white cloth.

Tuesday

John says, 'There's the man I told you about.'

Place Jesus with John.

Wednesday

Jesus asks, 'What do you want?'

Cut out the question mark from the template on page 85 and place it next to Jesus.

Thursday

John's followers go with Jesus.

Cut out footprint shapes from the template on page 85 and place them next to Jesus.

Friday

Andrew tells his brother about Jesus.

Cut out Andrew from the template on page 85, colour him in and place him on the cloth.

Saturday

Andrew brings his brother to Jesus.

Cut out Simon Peter from the template on page 85, colour him in and place him on the cloth.

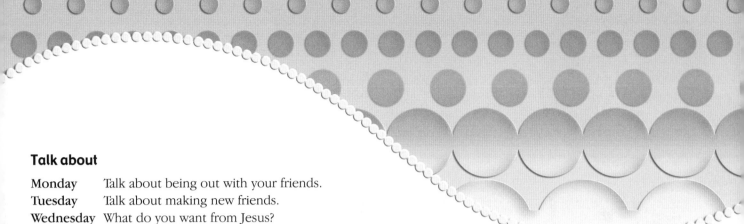

Talk about

Monday	Talk about being out with your friends.
Tuesday	Talk about making new friends.
Wednesday	What do you want from Jesus?
Thursday	What does it mean to follow Jesus?
Friday	What would you tell a friend about Jesus?
Saturday	Who would you like to bring to Jesus?

Prayer for the week

Loving God, John's friends followed Jesus. Help us to follow him too. Amen

Song for the week

Lamb of God (Tune: Three blind mice)
See page 58.

Year A

Second week of Epiphany

Tune: Three blind mice

There he is, there he is,
Lamb of God, Lamb of God.
The one I told you all about,
The one who will come after me.
For him I have prepared the way.
He'll save the world.

Andrew go, Andrew go,
Find Simon, find Simon,
And tell him you have seen the king,
And I have told you to follow him.
The time has come, you must leave me now,
And follow him.

Simon went, Simon went,
Andrew too, Andrew too.
These fishermen who left their nets,
They left their family and their friends
And went with Jesus on that day
And stayed with him.

Celebrating on Sunday

The second Sunday of Epiphany

Take to church

Take to church a footprint.

Sunday worship

For the minister or worship leader

> **You will need:**
> ✪ extra 'footprints' for everyone in the congregation

During the service

The minister or worship leader may explore and develop the talking points, then say the prayer for the week, inviting people to bring footprints to place on the cloth. The children may end this time by singing the song for the week (see page 58).

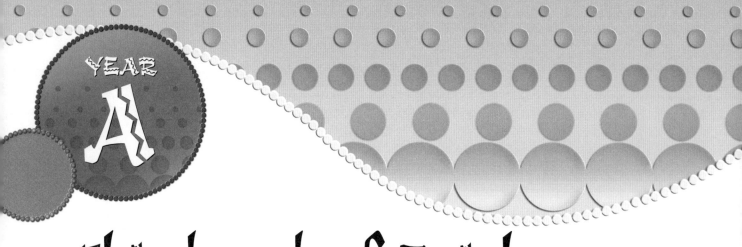

Third week of Epiphany

 Getting ready

 Let's play and pray...

Theme

Jesus chooses his first disciples

Bible focus

Jesus said to them, 'Come with me! I will teach you how to bring in people instead of fish.'

MATTHEW 4:19

Story for the week

One day, Jesus is walking by Lake Galilee when he sees Andrew and Simon Peter. They are both out on the lake, fishing with nets. Jesus calls out to them, 'Come with me! I will teach you how to bring in people instead of fish.' Andrew and Simon come in to shore, leave their nets and go with Jesus. They walk on and see their friends James and John, sitting mending their fishing nets. Jesus says, 'Come with me.' James and John leave their boats, their nets and their families, and they follow him. Jesus travels around, teaching about God and healing people.

Story cloth activities

Monday

Jesus is walking by Lake Galilee.

Cut out the Lake Galilee shape from the template on page 86, colour it in and place it on the cloth. Place Jesus by the lake.

Tuesday

Simon Peter and Andrew are fishing.

Cut out the fishing boat shape from the template on page 87, colour it in and place it on the lake.

Wednesday

Jesus says, 'I will teach you how to bring in people instead of fish.'

Make some circle shapes into faces and place them next to Jesus.

Thursday

Simon Peter and Andrew leave their boats and follow Jesus.

Move Jesus and the disciples away from the lake.

Friday

James and John give up everything to follow Jesus.

Cut out James and John shapes from the templates on page 86, colour them in and place them with Jesus and the others.

Saturday

Jesus travelled around, teaching and healing people.

Make some more circle shapes into faces and place them next to Jesus.

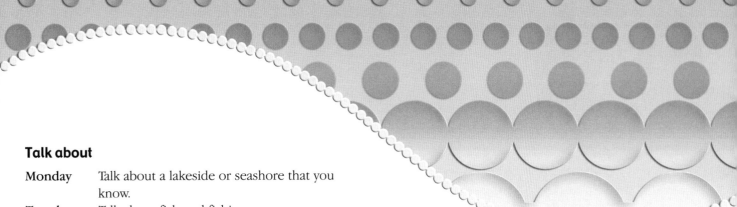

Talk about

Monday	Talk about a lakeside or seashore that you know.
Tuesday	Talk about fish and fishing.
Wednesday	I wonder what Jesus means when he says, 'I will help you to bring in people instead of fish.'
Thursday	Have you ever followed someone?
Friday	Talk about giving things up for friends.
Saturday	Imagine sitting in a crowd and listening to Jesus.

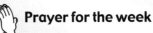 **Prayer for the week**

Loving God, Jesus sent his disciples out to tell others about you. Help us to do the same. Amen

Song for the week

Jesus walking on the shore (Tune: Humpty Dumpty) *See page 59.*

———— Year A ————

Third week of Epiphany

Tune: Humpty Dumpty

Jesus walking on the shore
By the lake of Galilee
Saw some fishermen nearby.
He raised his voice and gave a cry.
He raised his voice and gave a cry.

'Leave your nets behind,' he said.
'Come and fish for people instead.
Leave your nets and follow me.
My disciples you must be.
My disciples you must be.'

 ## Celebrating on Sunday

....

The third Sunday of Epiphany

Take to church

Take to church one of the face shapes.

Sunday worship

For the minister or worship leader

You will need:
✪ extra face shapes for everyone in the congregation

During the service

The minister or worship leader may explore and develop the talking points, then say the prayer for the week, inviting people to bring face shapes to place on the cloth. The children may end this time by singing the song for the week (see page 59).

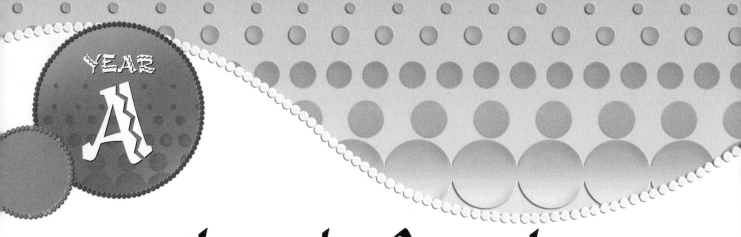

Fourth week of Epiphany

 ## Getting ready

This week may not always need to be used.

Theme

Jesus performs his first miracle

Bible focus

This was Jesus' first miracle, and he did it in the village of Cana in Galilee. There Jesus showed his glory, and his disciples put their faith in him.
JOHN 2:11

Story for the week

Jesus is at a wedding in Cana with his friends. Mary, his mother, is there too. In the middle of the feast, Mary comes to tell Jesus that there is no wine left for the wedding guests. Jesus tells the servants to fill up the six large water jars that are standing by the door. The man in charge tastes the water and calls across to the groom, 'You have kept the best wine until now!' The disciples are amazed that Jesus has turned the water into wine. Jesus has shown his glory and they all put their faith in him.

 ## Let's play and pray...

 Story cloth activities

Monday
Jesus is at a wedding feast in Cana.
  Remove the boat and the lake. Twist some foil into a wedding ring shape and place it next to Jesus.

Tuesday
Mary tells Jesus that there is no wine left for the wedding guests.
  Move Mary next to Jesus.

Wednesday
Jesus tells the servants to fill the jars with water.
  Cut out the water jars from the template on page 87 and place them next to Jesus.

Thursday
The water turns into wine.
  Colour the wine in the water jars.

Friday
Jesus shows his glory.
  Cut a circle of foil and place it in the centre of the cloth. Place Jesus in the centre of the foil circle.

Saturday
His disciples put their faith in Jesus.
  Make a big circle of all the people around Jesus.

Talk about

Monday	Talk about going to weddings.
Tuesday	What is it like to run out of something?
Wednesday	Talk about how water is stored.
Thursday	I wonder what the wedding guests thought about the water turning into wine.
Friday	Talk about how Jesus shows his glory.
Saturday	What do you think 'faith' means?

 Prayer for the week

Loving God, Jesus showed the people his glory at Cana. Help us to see his glory too. Amen

Song for the week

At a wedding in Cana (Tune: Away in a manger)
See page 60.

— Year A —

Fourth week of Epiphany

Tune: Away in a manger

At a wedding in Cana
While Jesus was there,
All the guests were unhappy
For the tables were bare.
The wine vat was empty
And the shops were all shut.
There'd be no celebration
With an empty wine cup.

There was plenty of water
But they'd run out of wine.
More guests were arriving
So they'd run out of time.
At some large jars of water
Jesus started to think.
'Take this cup to your master
And give him a drink.'

The master he tasted
And then gave out a gasp.
'This wine is delicious,
It's the best kept till last.'
There were six jars of wine now
Where the water had been
At the wedding in Cana
In old Galilee.

 Celebrating on Sunday

The fourth Sunday of Epiphany

Take to church

Take to church the water jar shapes.

Sunday worship

For the minister or worship leader

You will need:
✪ extra water jar shapes for everyone in the congregation

During the service

The minister or worship leader may explore and develop the talking points, then say the prayer for the week, inviting people to bring the water jar shapes to place on the cloth. The children may end this time by singing the song for the week (see page 60).

33

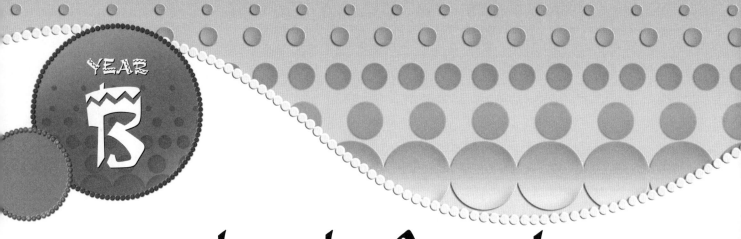

Second week of Epiphany

 ## Getting ready

Theme

Philip takes Nathanael to meet Jesus

Bible focus

Jesus said to Philip, 'Come with me.' Philip then found Nathanael and said, 'We have found the one that Moses and the Prophets wrote about. He is Jesus, the son of Joseph from Nazareth.'

JOHN 1:44b–45

Story for the week

One day, Jesus goes to Galilee, where he meets Philip. He says to Philip, 'Come with me!' Philip then goes to look for his friend Nathanael and finds him sitting under a fig tree. He says, 'Nathanael, we have found the Messiah. He is Jesus, the son of Joseph from Nazareth.' At first, Nathanael says, 'Can anything good come from Nazareth?' but Philip replies, 'Come and see!' So Nathanael goes with Philip to meet Jesus. When Nathanael sees Jesus, he knows who he is. He says to Jesus, 'You are the Son of God and the king of Israel.'

 ## Let's play and pray...

 ### Story cloth activities

Monday

Jesus goes to Galilee.

Put the white cloth next to the other two cloths. Place Jesus on the white cloth.

Tuesday

Jesus says to Philip, 'Come with me.'

Cut out Philip from the template on page 88, colour him in and place him on the cloth next to Jesus.

Wednesday

Philip finds Nathanael sitting under a fig tree.

Cut out Nathanael and the fig tree from the templates on pages 88 and 89, colour them in and place them on the edge of the cloth.

Thursday

Philip tells Nathanael all about Jesus.

Put Philip with Nathanael so that they can talk.

Friday

Nathanael goes to meet Jesus.

Move Nathanael and Philip to Jesus. Take the fig tree away.

Saturday

Nathanael says to Jesus, 'You are the Son of God and the King of Israel.'

Cut out the crown from the template on page 88 and place it next to Jesus.

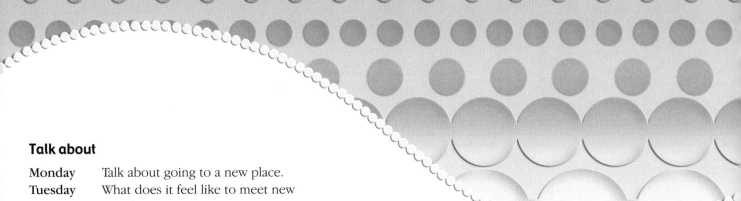

Talk about

Monday	Talk about going to a new place.
Tuesday	What does it feel like to meet new people?
Wednesday	Talk about sharing good news with friends.
Thursday	I wonder what Philiip said about Jesus.
Friday	I wonder what it is like to meet Jesus.
Saturday	Think of the names we give Jesus.

 Prayer for the week

Loving God, Jesus invited his friends to follow him. Help us to be your friends, too, and tell others about you. Amen

Song for the week

Philip found Nathanael (Tune: Here we go round the mulberry bush)
See page 61.

─── Year B ───

Second week of Epiphany

Tune: Here we go round the mulberry bush

Philip found Nathanael,
Nathanael, Nathanael.
Philip found Nathanael
And told him they'd seen Jesus.

He's the one that scripture says,
scripture says, scripture says,
He's the one that scripture says
Would come as the Messiah.

And now he's come from Nazareth,
Nazareth, Nazareth,
And now he's come from Nazareth.
He is the son of Joseph.

But he can't be from Nazareth,
Nazareth, Nazareth,
But he can't be from Nazareth.
No good can come from that place.

So Philip said, 'Well come and see,
come and see, come and see.'
So Philip said, 'Well come and see
And I will show you Jesus.'

Jesus knew Nathanael,
Nathanael, Nathanael.
Jesus knew Nathanael.
He'd seen him by the fig tree.

Nathanael saw and he believed,
he believed, he believed.
Nathanael saw and he believed
In Jesus, the Messiah.

Celebrating on Sunday

The second Sunday of Epiphany

Take to church

Take to church the crown.

Sunday worship

For the minister or worship leader

You will need:
✪ extra crowns for everyone in the congregation

During the service

The minister or worship leader may explore and develop the talking points, then say the prayer for the week, inviting people to place crowns on the cloth. The children may end this time by singing the song for the week (see page 61).

Third week of Epiphany

Getting ready

Theme

Jesus goes to a wedding at Cana

Bible focus

Mary then said to the servants, 'Do whatever Jesus tells you to do.'

JOHN 2:5

Story for the week

Jesus and his friends go to a wedding in a village called Cana. During the wedding feast, Jesus' mother, Mary, comes to tell him that the wine has run out. Mary says to the servants, 'Do whatever Jesus tells you to do.' Jesus asks the servants to fill up six stone jars with water and give some to the man in charge of the feast. The water has turned into wine and, when the man tastes it, he is amazed at how good it is. He says, 'It's the best wine I have ever tasted.' This is the first time that the disciples have seen Jesus' glory. They now know he is special and they believe in him.

Let's play and pray...

Story cloth activities

Monday

Jesus goes to a wedding.
  Make some confetti and place it around Jesus.

Tuesday

Mary and Jesus' friends are there too.
  Move Mary next to Jesus.

Wednesday

All the wine is gone.
  Make some sad face shapes.

Thursday

Jesus tells the servants to fill the stone jars with water.
  Cut out the stone jars from the template on page 89 and place them on the cloth.

Friday

The water turns into wine.
  Colour the stone jars.

Saturday

It was the best wine they had ever tasted.
  Turn over the sad faces and draw on happy faces.

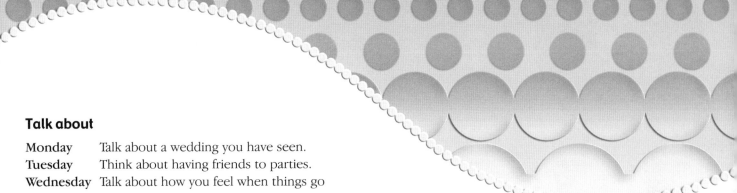

Talk about

Monday	Talk about a wedding you have seen.
Tuesday	Think about having friends to parties.
Wednesday	Talk about how you feel when things go wrong at a party.
Thursday	What might Jesus tell us to do?
Friday	What is it like to have a refreshing drink?
Saturday	Talk about leaving the best until last.

 Prayer for the week

Loving God, you always know what is best for us. Help us to remember this and always to do what Jesus wants. Amen

Song for the week

At a wedding in Cana (Tune: Away in a manger)
See page 62.

— Year B —

Third week of Epiphany

Tune: Away in a manger

At a wedding in Cana
While Jesus was there,
All the guests were unhappy
For the tables were bare.
The wine vat was empty
And the shops were all shut.
There'd be no celebration
With an empty wine cup.

There was plenty of water
But they'd run out of wine.
More guests were arriving
So they'd run out of time.
At some large jars of water
Jesus started to think.
'Take this cup to your master
And give him a drink.'

The master he tasted
And then gave out a gasp.
'This wine is delicious,
It's the best kept till last.'
There were six jars of wine now
Where the water had been
At the wedding in Cana
In old Galilee.

Celebrating on Sunday

The third Sunday of Epiphany

Take to church

Take to church your confetti.

Sunday worship

For the minister or worship leader

You will need:
✪ extra little bags of confetti for everyone in the congregation

During the service

The minister or worship leader may explore and develop the talking points, then say the prayer for the week, inviting people to sprinkle confetti on the cloth. The children may end this time by singing the song for the week (see page 62).

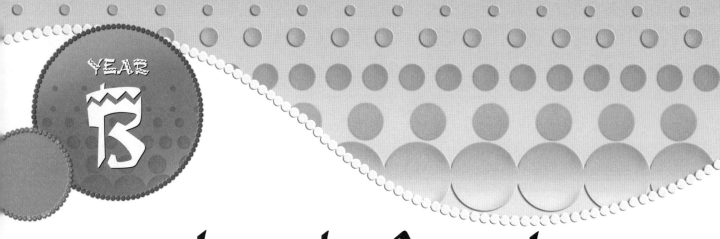

Fourth week of Epiphany

Getting ready

This week may not always need to be used.

Theme

Jesus heals a man with an evil spirit

Bible focus

'What is this? It must be some new kind of powerful teaching! Even the evil spirits obey him.'

MARK 1:27b

Story for the week

Jesus and his disciples are in Capernaum. On the sabbath, Jesus goes to the Jewish meeting place to teach. Everyone listens and is amazed at what he says. Suddenly Jesus is interrupted. A man with an evil spirit comes in and yells at Jesus, 'What do you want with us? Have you come to destroy us? I know who you are. You are God's Holy One!' 'Be quiet!' says Jesus. Then the man begins to shake and the evil spirit comes out of him with a loud scream. Everyone there is amazed. Jesus is the holiest man they have ever seen. Stories about Jesus quickly spread through Galilee.

Let's play and pray...

Story cloth activities

Monday

Jesus goes to the Jewish meeting place to teach.

Cut out the scrolls from the template on page 90 and place them by Jesus.

Tuesday

A man with an evil spirit yells at Jesus.

Cut out the man from the template on page 90, colour him in and place him on the cloth.

Wednesday

Jesus tells the evil spirit to leave the man.

Draw a happy face on the man.

Thursday

Everyone is really amazed.

Draw amazed faces on card circles and place them on the cloth.

Friday

Jesus is the holiest man they have ever seen.

Cut out a gold circle (halo) and place it behind Jesus' head.

Saturday

Stories about Jesus spread through Galilee.

Cut out arrow shapes and place them pointing outwards from Jesus.

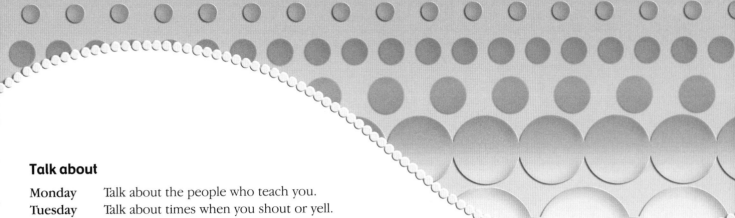

Talk about

Monday	Talk about the people who teach you.
Tuesday	Talk about times when you shout or yell.
Wednesday	Talk about the power of Jesus.
Thursday	What does it feel like to be amazed?
Friday	What does 'holy' mean?
Saturday	How can you tell others about Jesus?

Prayer for the week

Loving God, Jesus always helped those who came to him. Help us to care for other people. Amen

Song for the week

I know that you are Jesus Christ (Tune: The animals marched in two by two)
See page 63.

— Year B —

Fourth week of Epiphany

Tune: The animals went in two by two

'I know that you are Jesus Christ, the Son of God.
I know that you are Jesus Christ, the Son of God.
I know that you are Jesus Christ, the Son of God, the chosen one.
I know that I must trust and follow you.'

'Be quiet and come out of him, you evil one.
Be quiet and come out of him, you evil one.
Be quiet and come out of him.' The people were amazed because
The evil spirit did as it was told.

Wow! Evil spirits obey him, we are amazed.
Wow! Evil spirits obey him, we are amazed.
Wow! Evil spirits obey him, the greatest man there's ever been
For he is Jesus Christ, the Son of God.

🎈 Celebrating on Sunday

The fourth Sunday of Epiphany

Take to church

Take to church one of the amazed faces.

Sunday worship

For the minister or worship leader

You will need:
* extra amazed faces for everyone in the congregation

During the service

The minister or worship leader may carefully explore and develop the talking points, then say the prayer for the week, inviting people to bring the amazed faces to place on the cloth. The children may end this time by singing the song for the week (see page 63).

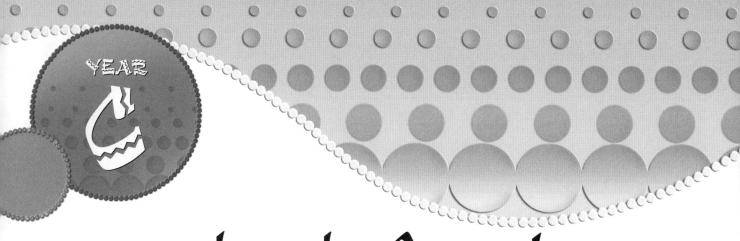

Second week of Epiphany

Getting ready

Theme

Jesus goes to a wedding

Bible focus

This was Jesus' first miracle, and he did it in the village of Cana in Galilee.

JOHN 2:11

Story for the week

Mary, Jesus and all the disciples are at a wedding in a village called Cana. Lots of people are there, enjoying themselves. Mary quietly says to Jesus, 'The wine has run out.' She sends the servants to Jesus and he says, 'Fill up those stone jars by the door with water.' They take some water from a jar to the man in charge of the feast, and he tastes it. The water has changed into good wine. The man in charge is surprised at how good it is. This is the first miracle that Jesus did and his disciples put their faith in him.

Let's play and pray...

Story cloth activities

Monday

Mary, Jesus and his disciples are at a wedding in Cana.

   Put the white cloth next to the other two cloths. Place Mary with Jesus.

Tuesday

Mary sends the servants to Jesus.

   Cut out some servant shapes from the template on page 92, colour them in and place them on the cloth.

Wednesday

Jesus tells the servants to fill the jars with water.

   Cut out the stone jars from the template on page 92 and place them on the cloth.

Thursday

The water turns into wine.

   Colour the stone jars.

Friday

This was Jesus' first miracle.

   Place the stone jars near Jesus.

Saturday

The disciples put their faith in Jesus.

   Cut out the disciples from the template on page 92, colour them in and place them near Jesus.

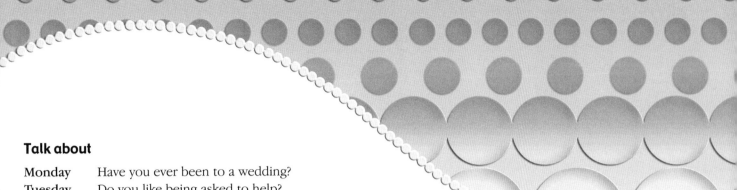

Talk about

Monday	Have you ever been to a wedding?
Tuesday	Do you like being asked to help?
Wednesday	What would you do if you ran out of food or drink at a party with your friends?
Thursday	I wonder what the people thought when the water turned into wine.
Friday	Were the people pleased that Jesus was at the wedding?
Saturday	Whom do you trust?

Prayer for the week

Loving God, you sent Jesus to show us great things. Help us always to trust in him. Amen

Song for the week

At a wedding in Cana (Tune: Away in a manger)
See page 64.

Year C

Second week of Epiphany

Tune: Away in a manger

At a wedding in Cana
While Jesus was there,
All the guests were unhappy
For the tables were bare.
The wine vat was empty
And the shops were all shut.
There'd be no celebration
With an empty wine cup.

There was plenty of water
But they'd run out of wine.
More guests were arriving
So they'd run out of time.
At some large jars of water
Jesus started to think.
'Take this cup to your master
And give him a drink.'

The master he tasted
And then gave out a gasp.
'This wine is delicious,
It's the best kept till last.'
There were six jars of wine now
Where the water had been
At the wedding in Cana
In old Galilee.

Celebrating on Sunday

The second Sunday of Epiphany

Take to church

Take to church a stone jar shape.

Sunday worship

For the minister or worship leader

You will need:
- ✪ extra stone jars shapes for everyone in the congregation

During the service

The minister or worship leader may explore and develop the talking points, then say the prayer for the week, inviting people to place the stone jar shapes on the cloth. The children may end this time by singing the song for the week (see page 64).

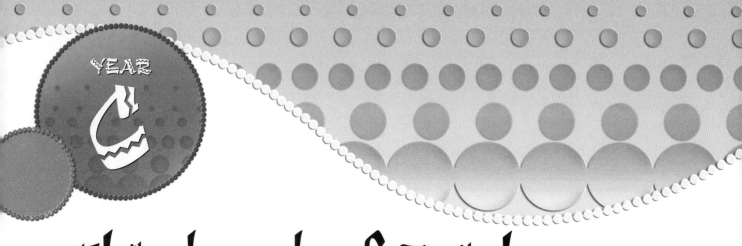

Third week of Epiphany

Getting ready

Theme

Jesus begins his work

Bible focus

Jesus returned to Galilee with the power of the Spirit. News about him spread everywhere. He taught in the Jewish meeting places, and everyone praised him.

LUKE 4:14–15

Story for the week

Jesus goes back home to the town of Nazareth, which is in the region of Galilee. On the sabbath, he goes to the Jewish meeting place. Jesus stands up to read the scriptures and is given a scroll with the words of the prophet Isaiah. He unrolls the scroll and reads, 'The Lord's Spirit has come to me, because he has chosen me to tell the good news to the poor. The Lord has sent me to announce freedom for prisoners, to give sight to the blind, to free everyone who suffers, and to say, "This is the year the Lord has chosen."' Jesus rolls up the scroll and hands it back to the man in charge. Then he says to everyone, 'What you have just heard me read has come true today.' Jesus is God's chosen one!

Let's play and pray...

Story cloth activities

Monday

Jesus goes home to Nazareth.

Cut out the Nazareth shape from the template on page 93, colour it in and place it on the edge of the cloth.

Tuesday

Jesus goes to a Jewish meeting place.

Cut out the meeting place shape from the template on page 93, colour it in and place it near Nazareth.

Wednesday

Jesus stands up in the meeting place.

Place Jesus on the meeting place shape.

Thursday

Jesus is given the Jewish scriptures to read.

Cut out the scroll from the template on page 93, roll it up and tie it with cord or ribbon. Place it by Jesus.

Friday

Jesus reads, 'God has chosen me to tell the good news.'

Open out the scroll and read the words.

Saturday

Jesus is God's chosen one.

Cut out the 'Chosen one' words from the template on page 93, colour them in and place them on Jesus.

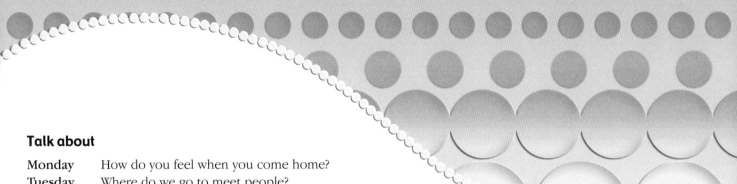

Talk about

Monday	How do you feel when you come home?
Tuesday	Where do we go to meet people?
Wednesday	Would you feel nervous about standing up in front of people you know?
Thursday	Think of some of the Bible stories you like to read.
Friday	How do we hear news?
Saturday	Talk about being chosen.

Prayer for the week

Loving God, you sent Jesus to tell us many important things. Help us to listen and obey his word. Amen

Song for the week

The Spirit of the Lord (Tune: Hokey cokey)
See page 65.

─── Year C ───

Third week of Epiphany

Tune: Hokey cokey

[musical notation]

The Spirit of the Lord
has come to me today.
The Spirit of the Lord
will give me many things to say.
He's chosen me to speak
and bring good news to the poor
And set his captives free.
Listen to the good news,
Listen to the good news,
Listen to the good news:
I am God's chosen one.

The Spirit of the Lord
has come to me today.
The Spirit of the Lord
will give me many things to say.
I am the very one
the prophets spoke about,
I'll make the blind to see.
Listen to the good news,
Listen to the good news,
Listen to the good news:
I am God's chosen one.

The Spirit of the Lord
has come to me today.
The Spirit of the Lord
will give me many things to say.
What you have heard me read today,
well now you know it's true,
I am God's chosen one.
Listen to the good news,
Listen to the good news,
Listen to the good news:
I am God's chosen one.

Celebrating on Sunday

The third Sunday of Epiphany

Take to church

Take to church the scroll shape.

Sunday worship

For the minister or worship leader

You will need:
✪ extra scroll shapes for everyone in the congregation

During the service

The minister or worship leader may explore and develop the talking points, then say the prayer for the week, inviting people to bring the scroll shapes to place on the cloth. The children may end this time by singing the song for the week (see page 65).

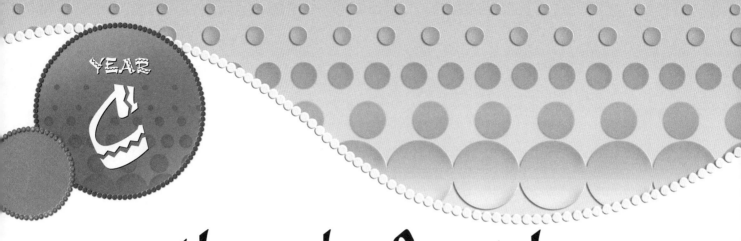

Fourth week of Epiphany

 **Getting ready**

 Let's play and pray...

This week may not always need to be used.

Theme

Everyone wants to see Jesus

Bible focus

'Come and see a man who told me everything I have ever done!'

JOHN 4:29a

Story for the week

Jesus is walking through Samaria, on his way to Galilee. He stops by a well for a drink of water, and a woman comes along. Now, Jewish people and people from Samaria don't speak to each other, but Jesus says to her, 'Please will you give me a drink of water?' As they talk, Jesus knows so much about her that the woman realizes that there is something very special about him. She recognizes that Jesus is the Messiah. She is so excited that she runs to tell her friends, 'Come and see a man who told me everything I have ever done.' Then they all come out of the village to meet Jesus.

 Story cloth activities

Monday

Jesus stops by a well for a drink.

Cut out the well shape from the template on page 94, colour it in and place it on the cloth. Place Jesus by it.

Tuesday

A woman from Samaria comes to the well.

Cut out the woman from the template on page 94, colour her in and place her by the well.

Wednesday

Jesus asks the woman for a drink of water.

Place a glass of water on the cloth.

Thursday

The woman realizes that Jesus is the Messiah.

Cut out and colour the word 'Messiah' from the template on page 94 and place it on the cloth next to Jesus.

Friday

The woman tells her friends about Jesus.

Cut out circles and draw faces on them.

Saturday

Everyone wants to meet Jesus.

Place all the faces on the cloth, in a circle around Jesus.

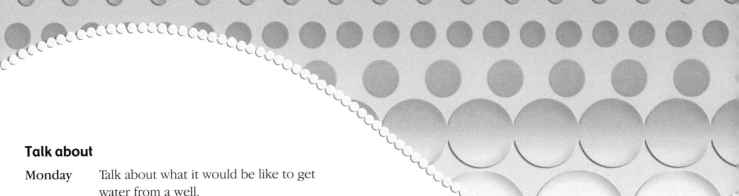

Talk about

Monday	Talk about what it would be like to get water from a well.
Tuesday	Talk about speaking to someone you don't like.
Wednesday	Talk about asking someone to help you.
Thursday	I wonder what 'Messiah' means.
Friday	Talk about telling people exciting news.
Saturday	Talk about meeting someone special.

Prayer for the week

Loving God, the woman from Samaria brought friends to meet Jesus. Help us to bring our friends to meet Jesus too. Amen

Song for the week

A woman standing all alone (Tune: Jack and Jill went up the hill)
See page 66.

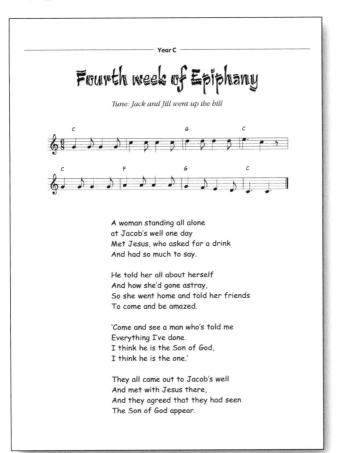

Celebrating on Sunday

The fourth Sunday of Epiphany

Take to church

Take to church the circle face shape.

Sunday worship

For the minister or worship leader

You will need:
✪ extra circle face shapes for the congregation

During the service

The minister or worship leader may carefully explore and develop the talking points, then say the prayer for the week, inviting people to bring the circle face shapes to place on the cloth. The children may end this time by singing the song for the week (see page 66).

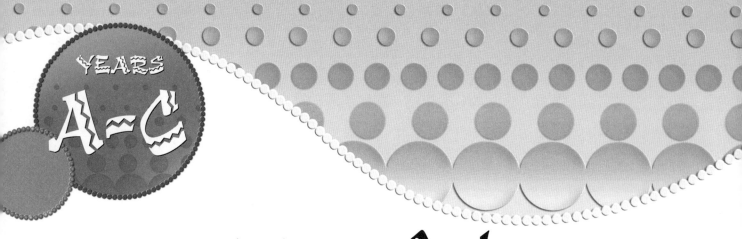

Presentation of Christ in the temple (Candlemas)

 ## Getting ready

Theme

Baby Jesus is taken to the temple

Bible focus

Simeon took the baby Jesus in his arms and praised God.

LUKE 2:28

Story for the week

Forty days after Jesus was born, Mary and Joseph take baby Jesus to the temple in Jerusalem so that they can present him to God. They take two doves to offer as a 'thank you' for their son. Two elderly people called Simeon and Anna are waiting there. Anna has lived in the temple for many years. God has promised Simeon that he will see Jesus before he dies. When Simeon sees the baby, he takes him in his arms and thanks God, saying, 'Lord, I can die in peace, because you have kept your promise. Jesus the Saviour is a light for all the people in the world.'

 ## Let's play and pray...

 ### Story cloth activities

Monday

Mary and Joseph go to the temple.

Cut out the temple shape from the template on page 95, colour it in and place it in the centre where the three cloths meet.

Tuesday

Mary and Joseph take Jesus to present him to God.

Place Mary, Joseph and the baby by the temple.

Wednesday

They bring two doves to say 'thank you' to God.

Cut out the two doves from the template on page 95, colour them in and place them next to Mary and Joseph.

Thursday

Simeon and Anna are waiting to see Jesus.

Cut out the Simeon and Anna shapes from the template on page 96, colour them in and place them by the temple.

Friday

Simeon takes the baby in his arms and sings a song of praise to God. Anna tells people about Jesus.

Cut out the music notes from the template on page 96 and place them next to Simeon.

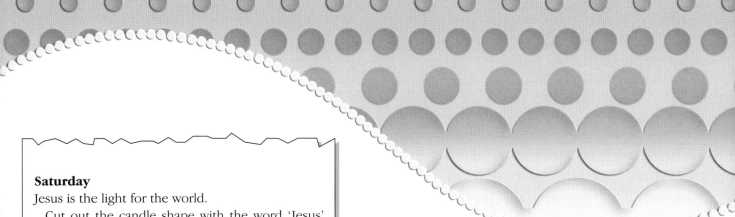

Saturday

Jesus is the light for the world.

Cut out the candle shape with the word 'Jesus' from the template on page 96, colour it in and place it on the temple.

Talk about

Monday	Talk about going to a place of worship.
Tuesday	Why did Mary and Joseph want to present Jesus to God?
Wednesday	Talk about how we say 'thank you' to God.
Thursday	What does it feel like to wait for things?
Friday	Do we sing when we are happy?
Saturday	Think about Jesus being the light for the world.

🙏 Prayer for the week

Loving God, you made Simeon and Anna happy because you promised that they would see Jesus. Help us to trust in your promises. Amen

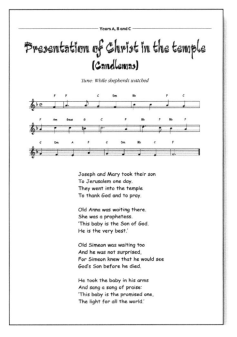

Song for the week

Joseph and Mary took their son (Tune: While shepherds watched) *See page 67.*

Celebrating on Sunday

The presentation of Christ in the temple

Take to church

Take to church the candle shape.

Sunday worship

For the minister or worship leader

You will need:
- ✪ extra candle shapes for everyone in the congregation

During the service

The minister or worship leader may explore and develop the talking points, then, say the prayer for the week, inviting people to bring the candle shapes to place on the cloth. The children may end this time by singing the song for the week (see page 67).

SONGS
for the week

First week of Advent

Tune: Jingle Bells

Wait with us, wait with us,
Wait with us and pray,
For we know the Son of God
Will come to us again.

Oh!
He is king, we will sing
On this happy day!
Wait with us, wait with us,
Wait with us and pray.

Sing with us, sing with us,
Sing with us today,
For we know the Son of God
Will come to us again.

Oh!
He is king, we will sing
On this happy day!
Wait with us, wait with us,
Wait with us and pray.

Second week of Advent

Tune: One man went to mow

Isaiah wrote a book, a long,
long time ago.
Isaiah wrote a book, a long,
long time ago.

A messenger, he said,
will come out from the desert.
A messenger, he said,
will come out from the desert.

The messenger will come
to clear the way for Jesus.
The messenger will come
to clear the way for Jesus.

'Get ready all,' he said,
for Jesus brings us good news.
'Get ready, all,' he said,
for Jesus brings us good news.

'We are sorry' they said,
'for the bad things we've done.'
'We are sorry,' they said,
'for the bad things we've done.'

Isaiah wrote a book, a long,
long time ago.
Isaiah wrote a book, a long,
long time ago.

Third week of Advent

Tune: London Bridge is falling down

What was John the Baptist like, Baptist like, Baptist like?
What was John the Baptist like? Tell me, please.

Does it matter that he ate, that he ate, that he ate,
Does it matter that he ate locusts 'n' honey?

From the desert land he came, land he came, land he came.
From the desert land he came to show the way to Jesus.

John the Baptist, he told us, he told us, he told us,
John the Baptist, he told us that Jesus is the light.

Fourth week of Advent

Tune: Frère Jacques

One day Mary, one day Mary was alone, was alone.
An angel came to see her, an angel came to see her
with some news, with some news.

Listen Mary, listen Mary. God is pleased, God is pleased.
You will have a baby, you will have a baby.
What great news, what great news!

Joseph's worried, Joseph's worried. What to do? What to do?
An angel came to see him, an angel came to see him
with some news, with some news.

Name him Jesus, name him Jesus. He's God's Son, he's God's Son.
His name means 'God is with us', his name means 'God is with us'.
What good news, what good news!

Week of Christmas

Tune: We wish you a merry Christmas

We're going to see a baby,
We're going to see a baby,
Yes we're going to see a baby,
And we're told he's a king!

He's lying in a manger,
He's lying in a manger,
Yes he's lying in a manger
In Bethlehem's town!

It seems like strange behaviour,
But the one we call the Saviour
Was a baby in a manger,
When he's really a king.

So let's sing out our praises
With the shepherds and the angels
For the child born in the stable,
Lord Jesus, our king.

Week after Christmas

Tune: There's a hole in my bucket

(Two-part song for Mary and the shepherds)

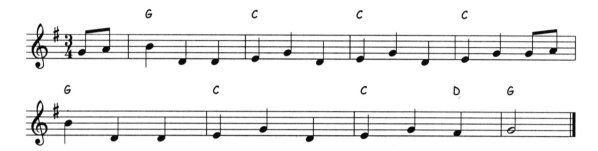

What's the name of your baby,
dear Mary, dear Mary?
What's the name of your baby,
dear Mary, what name?

We are calling him Jesus,
dear shepherds, dear shepherds.
We are calling him Jesus,
he's born to be king.

What a strange name to give him,
dear Mary, dear Mary.
What a strange name to give him.
Where did that come from?

From an angel named Gabriel,
dear shepherds, dear shepherds.
From an angel named Gabriel,
he gave me the name.

We have also seen angels,
dear Mary, dear Mary.
We have also seen angels
while watching our sheep.

You're the first to see Jesus,
dear shepherds, dear shepherds.
You're the first to see Jesus
asleep in the hay.

We'll all tell the good news,
dear Mary, dear Mary.
We'll all tell the good news that
we have seen the king.

Reproduced with permission from *Play and Pray through Advent* published by BRF 2008 (978 1 84101 567 5)

Week of Epiphany

Tune: Twinkle, twinkle little star

Option 1: The wise men visit Jesus

Wise men travelled from afar,
Led to Jesus by a star,
But King Herod scratched his head.
'There's no new king here,' he said.
So they went to Bethlehem
And knelt down and worshipped him.

That star helped them find the king
Gave their gifts and worshipped
him.
Then the wise men had a dream:
Herod is not what he seems.
Go back home another way,
Don't tell him where Jesus lay.

Week of Epiphany

Tune: The wheels on the bus

Option 2: Jesus is baptized in the River Jordan

Jesus came down from Galilee, Galilee, Galilee.
Jesus came down from Galilee
One fine day.

He said to John, 'Please baptize me, baptize me, baptize me.'
He said to John, 'Please baptize me',
One fine day.

Into the water Jesus went, Jesus went, Jesus went.
Into the water Jesus went
One fine day.

God's Spirit came down like a dove, like a dove, like a dove.
God's Spirit came down like a dove
One fine day.

God said, 'I'm pleased with my Son, with my Son, with my Son.'
God said, 'I'm pleased with my Son',
One fine day.

Second week of Epiphany

Tune: Three blind mice

There he is, there he is,
Lamb of God, Lamb of God.
The one I told you all about,
The one who will come after me.
For him I have prepared the way.
He'll save the world.

Andrew go, Andrew go,
Find Simon, find Simon,
And tell him you have seen the king,
And I have told you to follow him.
The time has come, you must leave me now,
And follow him.

Simon went, Simon went,
Andrew too, Andrew too.
These fishermen who left their nets,
They left their family and their friends
And went with Jesus on that day
And stayed with him.

Third week of Epiphany

Tune: Humpty Dumpty

Jesus walking on the shore
By the lake of Galilee
Saw some fishermen nearby.
He raised his voice and gave a cry.
He raised his voice and gave a cry.

'Leave your nets behind,' he said.
'Come and fish for people instead.
Leave your nets and follow me.
My disciples you must be.
My disciples you must be.'

Fourth week of Epiphany

Tune: Away in a manger

At a wedding in Cana
While Jesus was there,
All the guests were unhappy
For the tables were bare.
The wine vat was empty
And the shops were all shut.
There'd be no celebration
With an empty wine cup.

There was plenty of water
But they'd run out of wine.
More guests were arriving
So they'd run out of time.
At some large jars of water
Jesus started to think.
'Take this cup to your master
And give him a drink.'

The master he tasted
And then gave out a gasp.
'This wine is delicious,
It's the best kept till last.'
There were six jars of wine now
Where the water had been
At the wedding in Cana
In old Galilee.

Second week of Epiphany

Tune: Here we go round the mulberry bush

Philip found Nathanael,
Nathanael, Nathanael.
Philip found Nathanael
And told him they'd seen Jesus.

So Philip said, 'Well come and see,
come and see, come and see.'
So Philip said, 'Well come and see
And I will show you Jesus.'

He's the one that scripture says,
scripture says, scripture says,
He's the one that scripture says
Would come as the Messiah.

Jesus knew Nathanael,
Nathanael, Nathanael.
Jesus knew Nathanael.
He'd seen him by the fig tree.

And now he's come from Nazareth,
Nazareth, Nazareth,
And now he's come from Nazareth.
He is the son of Joseph.

Nathanael saw and he believed,
he believed, he believed.
Nathanael saw and he believed
In Jesus, the Messiah.

But he can't be from Nazareth,
Nazareth, Nazareth,
But he can't be from Nazareth.
No good can come from that place.

Third week of Epiphany

Tune: Away in a manger

At a wedding in Cana
While Jesus was there,
All the guests were unhappy
For the tables were bare.
The wine vat was empty
And the shops were all shut.
There'd be no celebration
With an empty wine cup.

There was plenty of water
But they'd run out of wine.
More guests were arriving
So they'd run out of time.
At some large jars of water
Jesus started to think.
'Take this cup to your master
And give him a drink.'

The master he tasted
And then gave out a gasp.
'This wine is delicious,
It's the best kept till last.'
There were six jars of wine now
Where the water had been
At the wedding in Cana
In old Galilee.

Fourth week of Epiphany

Tune: The animals went in two by two

'I know that you are Jesus Christ, the Son of God.
I know that you are Jesus Christ, the Son of God.
I know that you are Jesus Christ, the Son of God, the chosen one.
I know that I must trust and follow you.'

'Be quiet and come out of him, you evil one.
Be quiet and come out of him, you evil one.
Be quiet and come out of him.' The people were amazed because
The evil spirit did as it was told.

Wow! Evil spirits obey him, we are amazed.
Wow! Evil spirits obey him, we are amazed.
Wow! Evil spirits obey him, the greatest man there's ever been
For he is Jesus Christ, the Son of God.

Second week of Epiphany

Tune: Away in a manger

At a wedding in Cana
While Jesus was there,
All the guests were unhappy
For the tables were bare.
The wine vat was empty
And the shops were all shut.
There'd be no celebration
With an empty wine cup.

There was plenty of water
But they'd run out of wine.
More guests were arriving
So they'd run out of time.
At some large jars of water
Jesus started to think.
'Take this cup to your master
And give him a drink.'

The master he tasted
And then gave out a gasp.
'This wine is delicious,
It's the best kept till last.'
There were six jars of wine now
Where the water had been
At the wedding in Cana
In old Galilee.

Third week of Epiphany

Tune: Hokey cokey

The Spirit of the Lord
has come to me today.
The Spirit of the Lord
will give me many things to say.
He's chosen me to speak
and bring good news to the poor
And set his captives free.
Listen to the good news,
Listen to the good news,
Listen to the good news:
I am God's chosen one.

The Spirit of the Lord
has come to me today.
The Spirit of the Lord
will give me many things to say.
I am the very one
the prophets spoke about,
I'll make the blind to see.
Listen to the good news,
Listen to the good news,
Listen to the good news:
I am God's chosen one.

The Spirit of the Lord
has come to me today.
The Spirit of the Lord
will give me many things to say.
What you have heard me read today,
well now you know it's true,
I am God's chosen one.
Listen to the good news,
Listen to the good news,
Listen to the good news:
I am God's chosen one.

Fourth week of Epiphany

Tune: Jack and Jill went up the hill

A woman standing all alone
at Jacob's well one day
Met Jesus, who asked for a drink
And had so much to say.

He told her all about herself
And how she'd gone astray,
So she went home and told her friends
To come and be amazed.

'Come and see a man who's told me
Everything I've done.
I think he is the Son of God,
I think he is the one.'

They all came out to Jacob's well
And met with Jesus there,
And they agreed that they had seen
The Son of God appear.

Presentation of Christ in the temple (Candlemas)

Tune: While shepherds watched

Joseph and Mary took their son
To Jerusalem one day.
They went into the temple
To thank God and to pray.

Old Anna was waiting there.
She was a prophetess.
'This baby is the Son of God.
He is the very best.'

Old Simeon was waiting too
And he was not surprised,
For Simeon knew that he would see
God's Son before he died.

He took the baby in his arms
And sang a song of praise:
'This baby is the promised one,
The light for all the world.'

CRAFTS
for the week

The following ideas are suggested for use with children in midweek clubs and junior church where the whole week's activities might be covered in one session.

First week of Advent

Jesus tells us to get ready

Cut angel shapes out of fondant icing and place them on biscuits.

Second week of Advent

A messenger is coming

Decorate a clean stone using poster paints or felt-tipped pens.

Third week of Advent

John tells about Jesus

Take a piece of paper and, using poster paints, make a rainbow pattern. Cover the whole picture with black wax crayon. Using a pencil, write the word 'Jesus' in the crayon and see the rainbow colours shine through.

Fourth week of Advent

Mary will have a baby

Using felt-tipped pens, crayons or paints, decorate paper to wrap a present.

Week of Christmas

Jesus is born

Make a nativity scene out of play dough. To make your own play dough, mix 450g flour, 100g salt and two teaspoons of cream of tartar with two teaspoons of cooking oil and approximately 470ml warm water. Add food colouring as desired.

Week after Christmas

Mary and Joseph name Jesus

Make a name plate for your bedroom door out of craft foam.

Week of Epiphany (Option 1)

The wise men visit Jesus

Make up a gift box and decide what you would put in it for the baby Jesus. The gift doesn't have to be an object or anything that can be bought in the shops.

Week of Epiphany (Option 2)

Jesus is baptized in the River Jordan

Using the template on page 84 as a guide, draw an outline dove shape on acetate with a permanent marker. Fill in the reverse side with torn-up pieces of white tissue paper.

Second week of Epiphany

John's disciples follow Jesus

Make friendship bracelets by plaiting wool.

Third week of Epiphany

Jesus chooses his first disciples

Either make a fish collage, covered with garden netting to look like a fishing net, or make a fishing game.

To make the game, cut fish shapes out of holographic paper and use paper fasteners for eyes. Make a simple fishing rod from a small garden cane. Tie a piece of string to the cane and attach a round magnet with a hole in it to the other end of the string. Place the fish inside a cardboard box and pull them out with the rod. If desired, the box can be painted to look like the sea.

Fourth week of Epiphany

Jesus performs his first miracle

Make a peg doll bride and groom out of wooden dolly pegs and fabric pieces. The fabric pieces can be cut to size and fixed on to the dolls with PVA glue. Use felt-tipped pens to draw in the features.

Presentation of Christ in the temple (Candlemas)

The baby Jesus is taken to the temple

Make candles out of cardboard rolls and give them paper flames.

Crafts for the week

First week of Advent

Jesus tells us to get ready

Make a crown out of card, decorate it and size it to fit your head, so that you can wear it as a reminder that Advent is a time when we get ready to celebrate the birth of God's baby king.

Second week of Advent

A messenger is coming

Using crayon on sandpaper, make a picture of John the Baptist in the River Jordan.

Third week of Advent

John tells about Jesus

Write the name 'Jesus' on a piece of yellow parchment paper. Roll up the piece of paper to make a scroll with the name 'Jesus' inside and tie the scroll up with ribbon.

Fourth week of Advent

Mary will have a baby

Make an angel out of a plain white paper cup. Use a gold (non-glass) bauble for the head, tinsel for the arms and a paper doily to make the wings.

Week of Christmas

Jesus is born

Cut a crib and baby from craft foam. Stick a magnetic strip on the back to make a fridge magnet. Think about the baby Jesus being born at Christmas when you see the magnet on your fridge.

Week after Christmas

Mary and Joseph name Jesus

Glue lolly sticks (or strips of card) together to make a star shape and decorate it with shiny star stickers. Hang up your star to get ready to follow the star of wonder.

Week of Epiphany (Option 1)

The wise men visit Jesus

Find Iran on a map of the Near East. Now find Bethlehem. On a piece of paper, draw a map of the wise men's journey.

Week of Epiphany (Option 2)

Jesus is baptized in the River Jordan

Using white card, cut out some clouds and a dove. To make a mobile, use a hole punch to make a hole at the top of each shape. Thread a length of white cotton through each hole and hang the shapes at different levels on to a garden cane. Hang a looped thread from the centre of the cane so that the mobile can be hung up.

Second week of Epiphany

Philip takes Nathanael to meet Jesus

Either do a bark rubbing by taping a piece of paper to a tree and rubbing it gently but firmly with the side of a crayon, or do leaf printing by placing leaves underneath a piece of paper and gently rubbing over them with the side of a crayon.

Third week of Epiphany

Jesus goes to a wedding at Cana

Make a pretend wedding cake. Using a strip of card approximately 15cm wide, measure it to fit round the circumference of a paper plate, allowing a 2cm overlap. Glue the card into a circle with PVA glue or a glue stick. Make small cuts, approximately 2cm deep, all around the base and the top of the card circle. Bend the top and bottom edges in. Glue the bottom of the circle to a paper plate. Glue the bent edges at the top of the circle and place a second plate over the glued edges. Use a silver felt-tipped pen to decorate and, if desired, tie ribbon around the cake.

Fourth week of Epiphany

Jesus heals a man with an evil spirit

Using a strip of mediumweight card, make a 'Jesus the healer' bookmark.

Presentation of Christ in the temple (Candlemas)

The baby Jesus is taken to the temple

Make a headband out of a piece of card, approximately 6cm wide and 30cm long. Cut candle shapes out of card (see template on page 96). Glue the candle shapes around the headband, leaving a 6cm gap at each end. Use a hole punch to make a hole in the middle of each narrow end of the strip of card. Thread shirring elastic through the holes and tie off at the correct length to fit the head.

Crafts for the week

First week of Advent

Jesus tells us to get ready

Make candle shapes out of play dough (see recipe on page 70). Make a hole to thread ribbon through and hang the candles on the Christmas tree.

Second week of Advent

The messenger is coming

Using the template on page 91, make a trumpet out of silver or gold card. Punch a hole in the top edge of the trumpet and thread with ribbon to hang on the Christmas tree.

Third week of Advent

John tells about Jesus

Make a John the Baptist mask out of a paper plate. Cut a shape along one edge of the plate to allow your mouth to be seen and cut out eyeholes in the correct position to allow you to see. Colour the mask, punch a hole in either side and thread with shirring elastic, measured to fit your head. Use the mask to remind you what John said about Jesus.

Fourth week of Advent

Mary will have a baby

Make a manger out of a clean margarine tub filled with yellow shredded paper or hay.

Week of Christmas

Jesus is born

Make a sheep from card and cotton wool.

Week after Christmas

Mary and Joseph name Jesus

Use a white candle to write the name 'Jesus' on a sheet of paper and paint over it.

Week of Epiphany (Option 1)

The wise men visit Jesus

Draw the wise men on black paper and fill in the background with glue. Cover the paper with sand and tip away the excess. This should leave you with a picture of the wise men on a background of sand.

Week of Epiphany (Option 2)

Jesus is baptized in the River Jordan

Ask children to draw around their hands on to white paper. Cut out the hand shapes and make a large dove by sticking them on to a large piece of blue card (to represent the sky).

Second week of Epiphany

Jesus goes to a wedding

Make a place setting for a wedding feast with a decorated place mat and place card, a wine glass made out of a yoghurt pot covered in foil, and paper flower decorations.

Third week of Epiphany

Jesus begins his work

Make a paper scroll out of a piece of A4 paper and stain it with cold tea to make it look old. Then write a coded message on it.

Fourth week of Epiphany

Everyone wants to see Jesus

Make chocolate Krispie 'well' shaped cakes. Put 75g butter, 100g golden syrup and 60g plain chocolate (broken into pieces) into a saucepan. Stir over a low heat until melted. Add 50g Rice Krispies and stir until the cereal is fully coated with the chocolate mixture. Place paper cases in a bun tray and fill the cases with the chocolate Krispie mix, making a hollow in the centre of each. Place in the fridge to set.

Presentation of Christ in the temple (Candlemas)

The baby Jesus is taken to the temple

Make a tealight candle holder out of air-dry clay.

TEMPLATES

First week of Advent

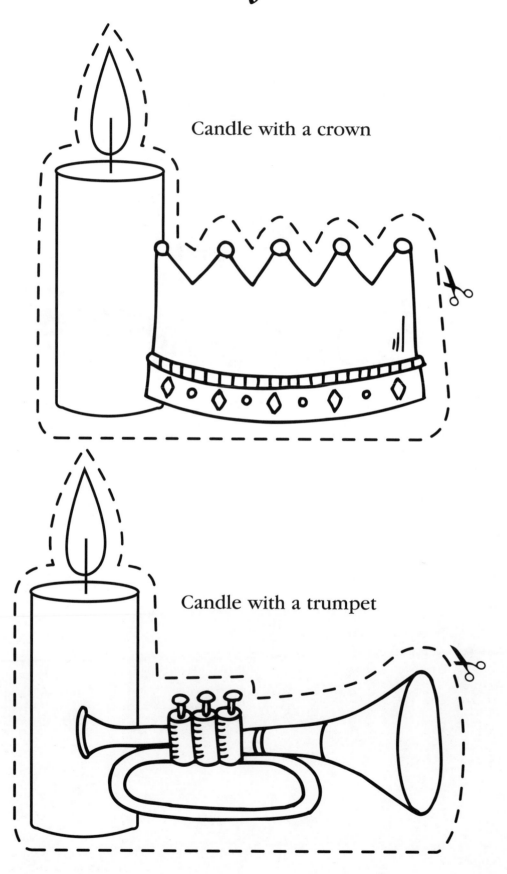

Candle with a crown

Candle with a trumpet

First week of Advent

Candle with an angel

Candle with
a scroll

Get ready

Second week of Advent

Open book

Messenger

Third week of Advent

John the Baptist

Fix tab to back of all card items to make them stand

Fourth week of Advent

Joseph   Mary

Week of Christmas

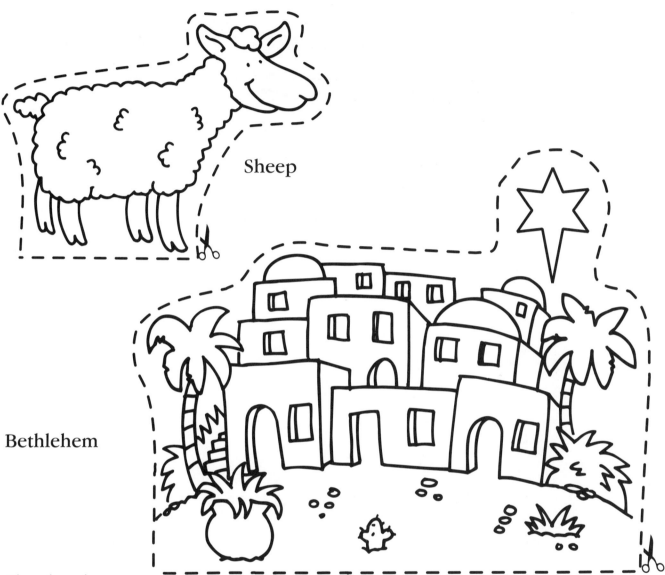

Sheep

Bethlehem

Shepherd

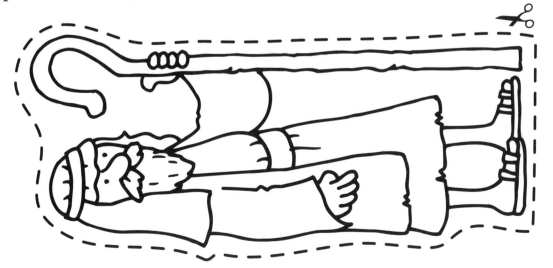

Week after Christmas

Baby Jesus

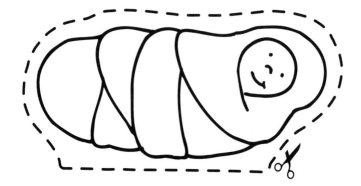

Week of Epiphany (Option 1)

Three wise men

Star

Gift shapes

Week of Epiphany (Option 2)

Dove

Jesus

Second week of Epiphany

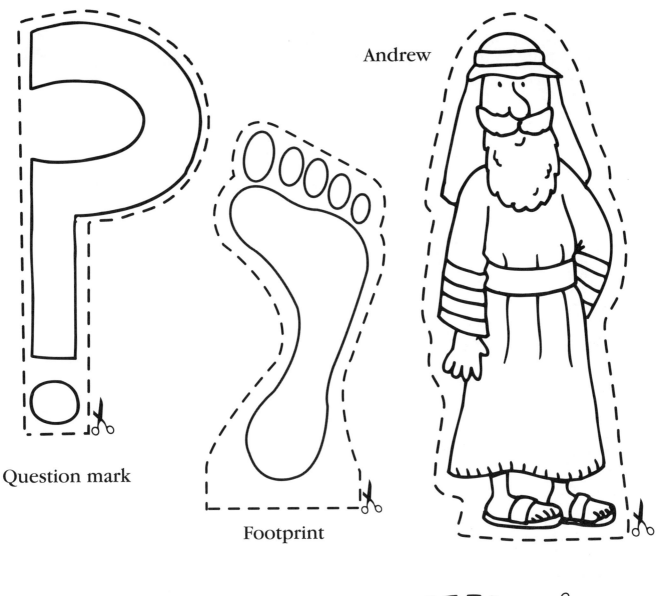

Question mark

Footprint

Andrew

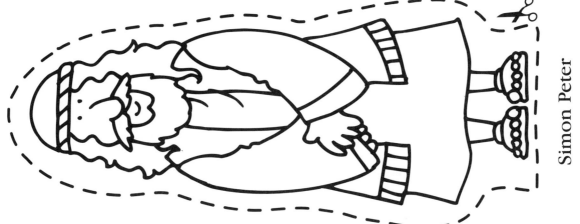

Simon Peter

Third week of Epiphany

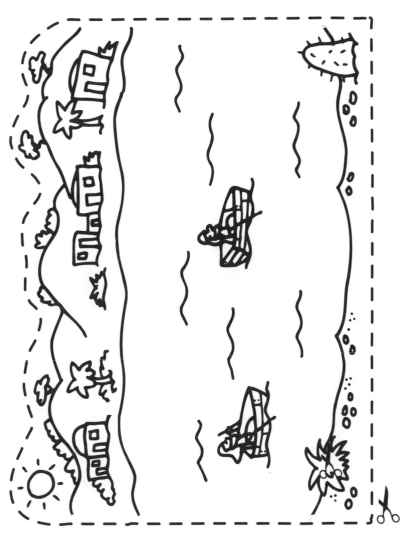

Lake Galilee

John

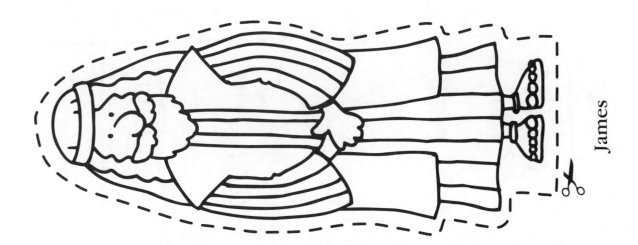

James

Third week of Epiphany

Fishing boat

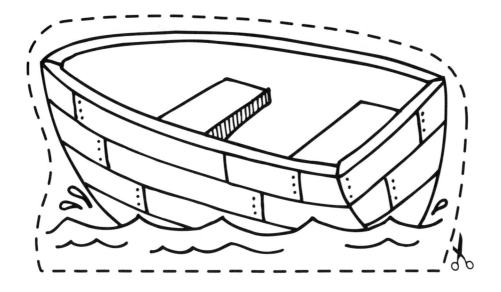

Fourth week of Epiphany

Water jars

Second week of Epiphany

Philip

Nathanael

Crown

Second week of Epiphany

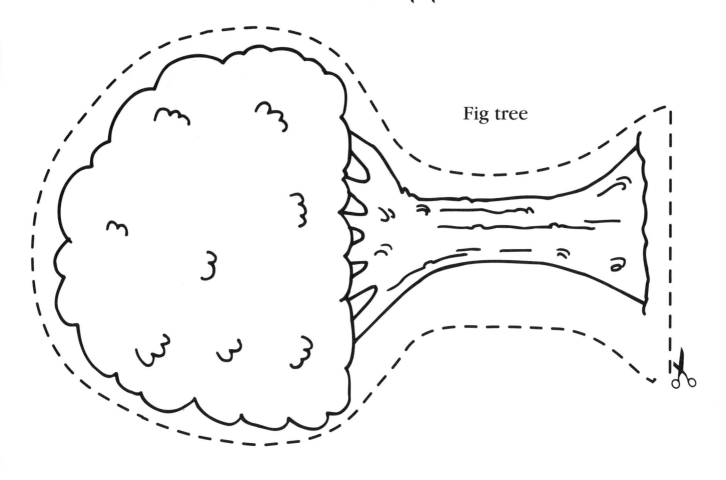

Fig tree

Third week of Epiphany

Six stone jars

Fourth week of Epiphany

Scroll

Man with an evil spirit

Second week of Advent

Craft for the week

The messenger is coming

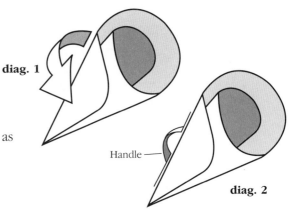

diag. 1

Cut out the trumpet template and shape into a cone, so that the straight edge forms the point and the curved edge forms the top as shown (diag. 1). Stick in place.

    Fix the two ends of the handle in place as shown (diag. 2).

Handle

diag. 2

Trumpet shape

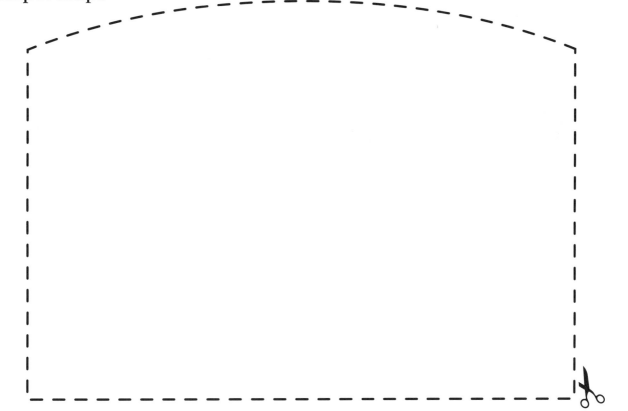

Handle shape

Second week of Epiphany

Six stone jars

Servant

Disciples

Third week of Epiphany

Chosen one

Nazareth

God has
chosen
me to
tell the
good news

Scroll

Meeting place

Fourth week of Epiphany

Well

Woman

Messiah

Presentation of Christ in the temple (Candlemas)

Two doves

Temple

Presentation of Christ in the temple

Musical notes

Simeon and Anna